The Benefits of

Bismillah

ir-Rahmaan ir-Raheem
& Surat al-Fatihah

The Benefits of

Bismillah

ir-Rahman ir-Raheem & Surat al-Fatihah

Shaykh Muhammad Hisham Kabbani

Published by the
Institute for Spiritual and Cultural Advancement

Published and Distributed by:

Institute for Spiritual and Cultural Advancement (ISCA)
17195 Silver Parkway, #201
Fenton, MI 48430 USA
Tel: (888) 278-6624
Fax: (810) 815-0518
Email: staff@naqshbandi.org
Web: http://www.naqshbandi.org

First Edition: October 2013
The Benefits of Bismillahi 'r-Rahmani 'r-Raheem & Surat al-Fatihah
ISBN: 978-1-938058-15-8

Library of Congress Cataloging-in-Publication Data

Kabbani, Muhammad Hisham.
The benefits of bismillahi 'r-rahmani 'r-raheem & surat al-fatihah
/ by Shaykh Muhammad Hisham Kabbani.
volumes cm
Includes bibliographical references.
ISBN 978-1-938058-15-8 (alk. paper)
1. Muhammad, Prophet, -632. 2. Naqshabandiyah. I. Title.
978-1-938058-15-8
297.6'3--dc23
2013013527

PRINTED IN THE UNITED STATES OF AMERICA
15 14 13 12 11 05 06 07 08 09

The author with his beloved master, His Eminence, Shaykh Muhammad Nazim Adil al-Haqqani. Cyprus, Sept. 2013.

Shaykh Kabbani giving a *suhbah,* an inspired spiritual discourse, in the renowned Naqshbandi *zawiya* in Michigan during the famed Ramadan Series of 2012. In 1990, after thirty years of training he was authorized by his master to teach Islamic spirituality (*tasawwuf*). July 2013.

Contents

About the Author ... i
Preface ... iii
Publisher's Notes ... v
Masters of the Naqshbandi-Haqqani Golden Chain ... ix
Recitation before Every Association ... xi
Some Benefits of Bismillahi 'r-Rahmani 'r-Raheem ... 1
The Key to the Heavenly Dome of the White Pearl ... 11
The Secrets of Alif and Ba ... 17
All Creation is within Muhammad ... 23
The Key to Open All Things is Knowledge of Ismullah al-`Azham ... 33
The Secret of Allah's Greatest Name ... 41
Seek Forgiveness and You Shall Be Forgiven ... 49
Each Verse of Surat al-Fatihah Closes One Door of Hellfire ... 57
The Fifteen Meems of Surat al-Fatihah ... 63
The Power of A`oodhu Billahi Min ash-Shaytani 'r-Rajeem ... 71
Allah's Protection ... 79
Islamic Calendar and Holy Days ... 87
Glossary ... 91
Other Publications ... 101

About the Author

World-renowned religious scholar Shaykh Muhammad Hisham Kabbani is featured in the ground-breaking book published by Georgetown University, *The 500 Most Influential Muslims in the World*. For decades, he has promoted traditional Islamic principles of peace, tolerance, love, compassion and brotherhood, while rigorously opposing extremism in all its forms. He hails from a respected family of traditional Islamic scholars, which includes the former head of the Association of Muslim Scholars of Lebanon and the present grand mufti (highest Islamic religious authority) of Lebanon.

Shaykh Kabbani is highly trained, both as a western scientist and as an Islamic scholar. He received a Bachelor's degree in Chemistry and later studied medicine. Under the instruction of Shaykh 'AbdAllah ad-Daghestani of Damascus (d. 1973), he holds a degree in Islamic Divine Law. Shaykh Muhammad Nazim Adil al-Haqqani, world leader of the Naqshbandi-Haqqani Sufi Order, authorized him to teach and counsel students in Sufism.

In his long-standing effort to promote a better understanding of traditional Islam, in February 2010, Shaykh Kabbani hosted HRH Charles, the Prince of Wales at a cultural event at the revered Old Trafford Stadium in Manchester, U.K. He has hosted two international conferences in the U.S., and regional conferences on a host of contemporary issues that attracted moderate Muslim scholars from Asia, the Far East, Middle East, Africa, U.K. and Eastern Europe. His counsel is sought by media outlets, academics, policymakers and government leaders.

For thirty years, Shaykh Kabbani has consistently promoted peaceful cooperation among people of all beliefs. Since the early 1990s, he launched numerous endeavors to bring moderate Muslims into the mainstream. Often at great personal risk, he has been instrumental in awakening Muslim social consciousness regarding the religious duty to stand firm against extremism and terrorism, for the benefit of all. His bright, hopeful outlook, with a goal to honor and serve all humanity has helped millions understand the difference between moderate mainstream Muslims and minority extremist sects.

In the United States, Shaykh Kabbani serves as Chairman, Islamic Supreme Council of America; Founder, Naqshbandi Sufi Order of America; Advisor, World Organization for Resource Development and Education; Chairman, As-*Sunnah* Foundation of America; Founder, *The Muslim Magazine*. In the United Kingdom, Shaykh Kabbani is an advisor to Sufi Muslim Council, which consults to the British government on public policy and social and religious issues.

Other titles by Shaykh Kabbani include: *The Importance of Prophet Muhammad in Our Daily Life* (2013), *The Dome of Provisions* (2013), *The Hierarchy of Saints* (2013, also in French), *Healing Verses in the Holy Qur'an and Sunnah* (2013), *Salawat of Tremendous Blessings* (2012, also in Turkish/Spanish), *The Heavenly Power of Divine Obedience and Gratitude* (2012), The Sufilive Series (2010-2012), *The Prohibition of Domestic Violence in Islam* (2011, also in French, Spanish), *At the Feet of My Master* (2010), *The Nine-fold Ascent* (2009), *Banquet for the Soul* (2008), *Illuminations* (2007), *Universe Rising* (2007), *Symphony of Remembrance* (2007), *A Spiritual Commentary on the Chapter of Sincerity* (2006), *The Sufi Science of Self-Realization* (Fons Vitae, 2005), *Keys to the Divine Kingdom* (2005), *Classical Islam and the Naqshbandi Sufi Order* (2004), *The Naqshbandi Sufi Tradition Guidebook* (2004), *The Approach of Armageddon? An Islamic Perspective* (2003), *Encyclopedia of Muḥammad's Women Companions and the Traditions They Related* (1998, with Dr. Laleh Bakhtiar), *Encyclopedia of Islamic Doctrine* (7 vols. 1998), *Angels Unveiled* (1996), *The Naqshbandi Sufi Way* (1995), and *Remembrance of God Liturgy of the Sufi Naqshbandi Masters* (1994).

Preface

This book is based on the *suḥbah*, extemporaneous, divinely inspired discourses, of Shaykh Muhammad Hisham Kabbani, disciple and representative of the global head of the Naqshbandi-Haqqani Sufi Order, Mawlana Shaykh Muhammad Nazim Adil al-Haqqani of Cyprus. Their uplifting discourses often include anecdotes of venerable Sufi masters from the renowned Naqshbandi Golden Chain, which dates back to Prophet Muḥammad ﷺ.

The Benefits of Bismillah 'ir-Rahman 'ir-Raheem & Surat al-Fatihah is part of Ramadan Series 2012 and is based on advanced teachings of eminent Islamic scholars and Sufi masters. It details ancient wisdom of God's preference to be known and called upon by His Holy Names *Ar-Rahman*, The Most Beneficent, and *Ar-Raheem*, The Most Merciful, and their immense spiritual blessing. In addition, powerful benefits of *Surat al-Fatihah*, the most read chapter of Holy Qur'an that is recited in every Muslim prayer, are examined.

For fifty years, the author has sought to serve his master and promote these ancient teachings for the good of all, a spirit we hope is reflected in this book. These universal lessons will make a fine addition to any study of Islam, Prophet Muḥammad, Sufism, Islamic mysticism (Sufism), spirituality and New Age teachings.

Publisher's Notes

This book is directed to those familiar with the Sufi Way; however, to accommodate lay readers unfamiliar with Sufi terminology and practices, we have provided English translations of Arabic texts and a comprehensive glossary. Where Arabic terms are crucial to the discussion, we have included transliteration and explanations. For readers familiar with Arabic and Islamic teachings, for further clarity please consult the cited sources.

The original material is based on transcripts of a series of holy gatherings known as *ṣuḥbah,* a divinely inspired talk given by the "Shaykh," a highly trained spiritual guide. To present the authentic flavor of such rare teachings, great care was taken to preserve the speaking styles of both the author and the illustrious shaykhs upon whose notes this book is based.

Translations from Arabic to English pose unique challenges that we have tried our best to make understandable to Western readers. Please note our application of the common Arabic oral tradition of omitting definite articles such as "the Prophet" and "the Holy Qur'an," as practiced by Muslims around the world as intimate references.

We apply contemporary American English publishing standards and italicize foreign proper nouns (*Fātiḥah, Quṭb az-Zamān, Rasūlullāh, Sūratu 'n-Naml),* but not commonly known foreign-language nouns (jihād, Qur'an, shaykh) unless they appear in transliterations.

Quotes from the Holy Qur'an and Holy Traditions of Prophet Muḥammad are offset, italicized and cited.

The pronoun "they" is frequently used by Sufi guides to reference heavenly beings and holy souls who support them and give them orders, a usage that appears throughout this book. Where gender-specific pronouns such as "he" and "him" are applied in a general sense, no discrimination is intended towards women, upon whom The Almighty bestowed great honor.

Islamic teachings are primarily based on four sources, in this order:

- **Holy Qur'an**: the Islamic holy book of divine revelation (God's Word) granted to Prophet Muḥammad. Reference to Holy Qur'an appears as "4:12," which indicates "Chapter 4, Verse 12."

- *Sunnah*: holy traditions of Prophet Muḥammad ﷺ; the systematic recording of his words and actions that comprise the *ḥadīth*. For fifteen centuries, Islam has applied a strict, highly technical standard, rating each narration in terms of its authenticity and categorizing its "transmission." As this book is not highly technical, we simplified the reporting of *ḥadīth*, but included the narrator and source texts to support the discussion at hand.
- *Ijma*ʿ: The adherence, or agreement of the experts of independent reasoning *(āhl al-ijtihād)* to the conclusions of a given ruling pertaining to what is permitted and what is forbidden after the passing of the Prophet, Peace be upon him, as well as the agreement of the Community of Muslims concerning what is obligatorily known of the religion with its decisive proofs. Perhaps a clearer statement of this principle is, "We do not separate (in belief and practice) from the largest group of the Muslims."
- **Legal Rulings:** highly trained Islamic scholars form legal rulings from their interpretation of the Qur'an and the *Sunnah*, known as *ijtihād*. Such rulings are intended to provide Muslims an Islamic context regarding contemporary social norms. In theological terms, scholars who form legal opinions have completed many years of rigorous training and possess degrees similar to a doctorate in divinity in Islamic knowledge, or in legal terms, hold the status of a high court or supreme court judge, or higher.

The following universally recognized symbols have been respectfully included in this work and are deeply appreciated by a vast majority of our readers:

ﷻ *Subḥānahu wa Taʿalā* (may His Glory be Exalted), recited after the name "Allah" and any of the Islamic names of God.

ﷺ *ṢallAllahu ʿalayhi wa sallam* (God's blessings and greetings of peace be upon him), recited after the holy name of Prophet Muḥammad.

عليه السلام *ʿAlayhi ʿs-salām* (peace be upon him/her), recited after holy names of other prophets, names of Prophet Muḥammad's relatives, the pure and virtuous women in Islam, and angels.

رضي الله عنه/عنها *RaḍīAllahu ʿanh(um)* (may God be pleased with him/her), recited after the holy names of Companions of Prophet Muḥammad; plural: *raḍīAllahu ʿanhum*.

ق Represents *QaddasAllahu sirrah* (may God sanctify his secret), recited after names of saints.

Transliteration

Transliteration from Arabic to English poses challenges. To show respect, Muslims often capitalize nouns which, in English, appear in lowercase.

To facilitate authentic pronunciation of names, places and terms, use the following key:

Symbol	Transliteration	Symbol	Transliteration	Vowels: Long	
ء	ʾ	ط	ṭ	آ ى	
ب	b	ظ	ẓ	و	
ت	t	ع	ʿ	ي	
ث	th	غ	gh	Short	
ج	j	ف	f	ـَ	
ح	ḥ	ق	q	ـُ	
خ	kh	ك	k	ـِ	
د	d	ل	l		
ذ	dh	م	m		
ر	r	ن	n		
ز	z	ه	h		
س	s	و	w		
ش	sh	ي	y		
ص	ṣ	ة	ah; at		
ض	ḍ	ال	al-/'l-		

Masters of the Naqshbandi-Haqqani Golden Chain

May Allah ﷻ preserve their secrets.

1. Prophet Muḥammad ibn ʿAbdAllah ﷺ

2. Abū Bakr as-Ṣiddīq ق
3. Salmān al-Farsi ق
4. Qasim bin Muḥammad bin Abū Bakr ق
5. Jafar aṣ-Ṣādiq ق
6. Tayfur Abū Yazīd al-Bistāmi ق
7. Abūl Hassan ʿAlī al-Kharqani ق
8. Abū ʿAlī al-Farmadi ق
9. Abū Yaqūb Yusuf al-Hamadani ق
10. AbūlAbbas, al-Khiḍr ق
11. ʿAbdul Khāliq al-Ghujdawani ق
12. Arif ar-Riwakri ق
13. Khwaja Maḥmūd al-Anjir al-Faghnawi ق
14. ʿAlī ar-Ramitani ق
15. Muḥammad Baba as-Samasi ق
16. as-Sayyid Amir Kulal ق
17. Muḥammad Bahaʿuddin Shah Naqshband ق
18. Alaʿuddin al-Bukhāri al-Attar ق
19. Yaqūb al-Charkhi ق
20. Ubaydullāh al-Aḥrar ق
21. Muḥammad az-Zahid ق
22. Darwish Muḥammad ق
23. Muḥammad Khwaja al-Amkanaki ق
24. Muḥammad al-Baqi billāh ق
25. Aḥmad al-Farūqi as-Sirhindi ق
26. Muḥammad al-Masum ق
27. Muḥammad Sayfuddin al-Farūqi al-Mujaddidi ق
28. as-Sayyid Nūr Muḥammad al-Badawani ق
29. Shamsuddin Habib Allah ق
30. ʿAbdAllah ad-Dahlawi ق
31. Khālid al-Baghdādī ق
32. Ismail Muḥammad ash-Shirwāniق
33. Khas Muḥammad Shirwāni ق
34. Muḥammad Effendi al-Yaraghi ق
35. Jamāluddin al-Ghumuqi al-Ḥusayni ق
36. Abū Aḥmad as-Sughuri ق
37. Abū Muḥammad al-Madani ق
38. Sharafuddīn ad-Daghestāni ق
39. ʿAbdAllah al-Faʿiz ad-Daghestāni ق
40. Muḥammad Nazim Adil al-Haqqani ق

Recitation before Every Association

بسم الله الرحمن الرحيم

A'ūdhu billāhi min ash-Shayṭān ir-rajīm.
Bismillāhi' r-Raḥmāni 'r-Raḥīm.
Nawaytu 'l-arbā'īn, nawaytu 'l-'itikāf,
nawaytu'l-khalwah, nawaytu 'l-'uzlah,
nawaytu 'r-riyāḍa, nawaytu 's-sulūk,
lillāhi Ta'alā fī hādhā 'l-masjid.

Ati'ūllāha wa ati' ūr-Rasūla
wa ūli'l-amri minkum.

I seek refuge in Allah from Satan, the Rejected.
In the Name of Allah, the Merciful,
the Compassionate.
I intend the forty (days of seclusion);
I intend seclusion in the mosque,
I intend seclusion, I intend isolation,
I intend discipline (of the ego); I intend to travel
in God's Path for the sake of God,
in this mosque.

Obey Allah, obey the Prophet,
and obey those in authority among you.
Sūratu 'n-Nisā (The Women), 4:59

Some Benefits of Bismillahi 'r-Rahmani 'r-Raheem

Aʿūdhu billāhi min ash-Shayṭāni 'r-rajīm. Bismillāhi' r-Raḥmāni 'r-Raḥīm.
Nawaytu 'l-arbāʿīn, nawaytu 'l-ʿitikāf, nawaytu'l-khalwah, nawaytu 'l-ʿuzlah,
nawaytu 'r-riyāḍa, nawaytu 's-sulūk, lillāhi Taʿalā fi hādhā 'l-masjid.
Atīʿūllāha wa atīʿū 'r-Rasūla wa ūlī 'l-amri minkum.
Obey Allah, obey the Prophet, and obey those in authority among you. (4:59)

Dastūr, madad yā Sulṭān al-Awlīyā, Mawlana Shaykh Nazim al-Haqqani ق.
Dastūr, madad yā Sulṭān al-Awlīyā, Mawlana Shaykh ʿAbdAllah ad-Daghestani ق.

A*llahumma salli `ala Sayyidina Muhammad, hatta yarda Sayyidina Muhammad! As-salaamu `alaykum wa rahmatullaahi wa barakaatuh.* It is a new day and a new page; every day is a page in our life. We don't want to lose these special moments in this house of Allah, so we try to sit together as much as we can.

أَطِيعُواْ اللّهَ وَأَطِيعُواْ الرَّسُولَ وَأُوْلِي الأَمْرِ مِنكُمْ

Ati`oollaha wa ati`oo 'r-Rasoola wa ooli 'l-amri minkum.

Obey Allah, obey the Prophet, and obey those in authority among you.

(Surat an-Nisa, 4:59)

Sayyidina Anas ibn Malik ؓ related that Prophet ﷺ said:

إذا مررتم برياض الجنة فارتعوا، قالوا: وما رياض الجنة؟ قال: حلق الذكر.

Wa idhaa ra'aytum riyaad al-Jannati farta`oo feehaa. qaaloo yaa Rasoolullah wa maa riyaadu 'l-Jannah. Qaaloo yaa Rasoolullah wa maa riyaadu 'l-Jannah. Qaala Rasoolullah hilaqu 'd-dhikr.

(O my Companions!) If you find the Heavenly Gardens on earth, stay there and sit in it and be in it. They asked, "What are these riyaadu 'l-Jannah that we must run to?" He said, "Associations of dhikrullah."

That is why we don't want to lose the meaning of that *hadith,* but we have to fulfill it as much as we can. Prophet ﷺ said, *wa idhaa ra'aytum riyaadu 'l-Jannah,* "If you pass through a group of people sitting like this, it is considered a *rawdah* from Paradise," meaning a quarter of *Jannah,* which is assigned to people. Sitting in a *masjid* or a house making *dhikrullah,* remembering Allah ﷻ and His Prophet ﷺ, and sitting and listening to each other is *rawdatu 'l-Jannah.* Everyone is killing themselves to reach *Madinatu 'l-Munawwara* to visit Prophet and to pray in *Rawdat an-Nabi* ﷺ. We try to go there because it is a piece of Paradise, but why? Did Allah bring a stone like *Hajar al-Aswad* there? No, it is because of the *barakah* of the feet of Prophet ﷺ: when they touched that place they turned it into a *rawdah* of Paradise. Prophet wants his *ummah* to be dressed with the secret of being in *dunya,* while in reality they are in Paradise!

So wherever and whenever these meetings happen, such as in *masajid* where people sit together making *dhikrullah,* it becomes a *rawdah* of *Riyaadu 'l-Jannah,* a place of peace and safety from Hellfire. So even if you sit in a place of *Riyaadu 'l-Jannah* once, do you think Allah ﷻ is going to put you in Hellfire after He dressed you with the manifestations and beautiful paradises of *Jannah*? No way! That is why Prophet ﷺ said, "Sit and graze," meaning, sit and eat from the manifestations of *dhikr,* from the Beautiful Names and Attributes, as you are remembering Allah ﷻ with these words.

O Muslims! *Hilaqu 'd-dhikr* and *dhikrullah* are mentioned in many *ahadith.* Anything that relates to *dhikrullah* is Heaven. If you read Qur'an or *ahadith,* make *salawaat,* recite the Beautiful Names and Attributes, or even if two people sit together in a *masjid* without saying anything, it is considered *dhikrullah* as their breath will become *dhikrullah*!

Imam Jalaluddin as-Suyuti ؓ, who wrote the first half of Tafsir al-Jalalayn, among many other books, was asked:

Regarding *dhikr* associations, is it accepted or *makhrooh,* disliked, to raise your voice loud when you are in a *masjid* and you say, "*SubhaanAllah, w 'alhamdulillah, wa laa illaha illa-Llah, w 'Allahu Akbar*?" He said, "There is no dislike in anything like that, but it is accepted and liked by Allah ﷻ and His Prophet ﷺ."[1]

Therefore, no one can say that *dhikrullah* is not allowed! Imam Suyuti, one of the big *`ulama* whose works they still study everywhere around the world, even in countries where they have their own *madhdhab,* said, "Allah

---

[1] Imam Suyuti, Kashf al-Kina`ah.

likes associations in which they do *dhikrullah,"* so that is clear for us, for the audience and all those who are listening. He also said there are so many *ahadith* about loud *dhikr* and one states that it is also liked for you to raise your voice when reciting Holy Qur'an. So when you are reading Holy Qur'an, you mention many times *suhbaanAllah, alhamdulillah,* "Allah" or "Muhammad," or Allah's Beautiful Names and Attributes are mentioned and we know Allah ﷻ said, "Call Me with these Beautiful Names and Attributes," whatever of these are mentioned in Holy Qur'an, you can add to your daily *wird* or recite some of these words in *jama`ah* and Allah likes that.

Imam Nawawi ؓ mentioned in his book Al-Adhkaar that to use a loud voice in *dhikrullah* is accepted in some areas more than the hidden (silent) *dhikr* is recommended. Therefore, we are quoting both *`ulama* in order to show that *dhikrullah* is accepted in whatever form you like. Is, *"Bismillahi 'r-Rahmaani 'r-Raheem"* mentioned in the Holy Qur'an or not? If we say, *"Bismillahi 'r-Rahmaani 'r-Raheem, Bismillahi 'r-Rahmaani 'r-Raheem, Bismillahi 'r-Rahmaani 'r-Raheem,"* what do we get?

Ibn Mas`ood ؓ, one of the greatest *Sahaabi* scholars, said:

> Whoever wants Allah ﷻ to save him from the nineteen angels who control Jahannam has to say, *"Bismillahi 'r-Rahmaani 'r-Raheem."* Allah will make every letter from *Bismillahi 'r-Rahmaani 'r-Raheem* a safety from these angels. If he was judged for punishment, these angels will take him out from Jahannam because he recited *"Bismillahi 'r-Rahmaani 'r-Raheem."*

Bismillahi 'r-Rahmaani 'r-Raheem has nineteen letters, and there are nineteen angels who guard Hellfire, so each letter of *Bismillahi 'r-Rahmaani 'r-Raheem* represents one angel and you are asking Allah to save you from Hellfire! If you look at the Holy Qur'an and *ahadith,* everything has a meaning and a sign. There are three places where everyone can see the relationship between calling Allah ﷻ through *Bismillahi 'r-Rahmaani 'r-Raheem* or calling Prophet ﷺ through certain names that he likes. *Bismillahi 'r-Rahmaani 'r-Raheem* equals the nineteen angels of Hellfire, which equals the nineteen letters that consist of *Ahlu 'l-`Abbaa,* the Family of the Prophet ﷺ, with whom the Prophet covered with his *jubbah* and said, "These are my family, don't hurt them." *Ahlu 'l-`Aabbaa* is comprised of the Prophet ﷺ, his daughter Fatimah ؓ, Sayyidina `Ali ؓ, Sayyidina Hassan ؓ and Sayyidina Husayn ؓ.

If you count the letters of their names it equals nineteen, and each letter of their names represents "*Bismillahi 'r-Rahmaani 'r-Raheem.*" "Muhammad" is comprised of four letters, "Fatimah" is five letters, etc., and if you add them it equals nineteen. *Bismillahi 'r-Rahmaani 'r-Raheem* equals nineteen letters and the angels of Hellfire are nineteen, so the *barakah* of Prophet and *Bismillahi 'r-Rahmaani 'r-Raheem* will save you from Hellfire! Therefore, *dhikr* is important in Islam, in spirituality, and for everyone to save themselves from Hellfire. Say "*Bismillahi 'r-Rahmaani 'r-Raheem*" as much as you can, and our teacher ordered us to recite it one-hundred times daily.

Now we will relate a *hadith* from Bukhari, because some people on the Internet say, "We only want *ahadith* from Imam Bukhari." Was Imam Bukhari the only person to relate *ahadith*? No, Prophet ﷺ used to speak with the young, the elders, everyone, and not all *Sahaabah* ؓ heard all *ahadith*! Imam Ahmad ibn Hanbal ؓ memorized 300,000 *ahadith* in more than fifty different categories! Never mind, we will recite a *hadith* from Bukhari:

Prophet said, "Allah has angels who roam the streets," just like your telephones use roaming technology, does Allah not have heavenly technology? *Kun fa yakoon*! Allah ordered angels to look for associations of *dhikr* like this one here. Angels are filling the place, though we cannot see them, the *imam* can see them and perhaps some of the viewers can see them; many people can see and many cannot. "*At-turuq*" has two meanings, one of which is "the street." "*At-tareeq*" is singular, "*at-turuq*" is plural, and it also means the Sufi Orders, that the angels are first going to the people of *Ahlu 'l-Tasawwuf* because they are the real *Ahlu 's-Sunnah wa 'l-Jama`ah* who love the Prophet ﷺ, who make *dhikr* and accept everything that shows the Greatness of Sayyidina Muhammad ﷺ!

وَأَلَّوِ اسْتَقَامُوا عَلَى الطَّرِيقَةِ لَأَسْقَيْنَاهُم مَّاءً غَدَقًا

Wa law istiqaamoo `alaa 't-tareeqati la-asqaynaahum maa'an ghadaqa.

If they had (only) remained on the (right) Way, We should certainly have bestowed on them rain in abundance. *(Surat al-Jinn, 72:16)*

It means, "If they keep on the Right Path, *Siraatu 'l-Mustaqeem*," and it also means, "If they keep on their *tareeqah*, under the guidance of their *shuyookh* in different *turuq*." There are many *turuq* with many *shuyookh* and each one has his own understanding and way that he feels Allah ﷻ has dressed him with, and we cannot deny that. There are forty-one main *tareeqahs* such as Chishti, Qadiri, Naqshbandi, Shadhili, and Muridiyya. We cannot deny any of them, and each one is guiding you to Allah ﷻ and to the door of Prophet ﷺ.

The angels are searching for people who are remembering Allah ﷻ. They found them here! Today we are here, but it might be that there are other people somewhere else. Even if there is one person on a mountain, they will find him because if someone is on a mountain making *dhikrullah,* angels will be there! If they find a group of people remembering Allah ﷻ, they say, "Come quickly! We must sit here!" and now they are sitting here among us. We don't see them, but they are here and we are being dressed with their presence, have no doubt! They wrap their wings around you, going up, up, up (if we can say "up," as there is no up or down in Heavens), and they encompass you in circles until they reach *as-samaa' ad-dunya.* The entire group of people is encircled by angels! Can you count how many angels that is? It's beyond the universe! Scientists found there are 60,000 galaxies and each galaxy has more than 80 billion stars, and yet this is still not the whole universe. We don't want to go into Physics now, but they go above that, where there is nothing except Heavens and their *dhikr* will be written for us.

عَنْ أبِي هُرَيْرَةَ رضي الله عنه قَالَ: قَالَ رَسُولُ اللَّهِ صلي الله عليه وآله وسلم: إنَّ لِلَّهِ مَلَائِكَةً يَطُوفُونَ فِي الطُّرُقِ، يَلْتَمِسُونَ أهْلَ الذِّكْرِ، فَإذَا وَجَدُوا قَوْمًا يَذْكُرُونَ اللَّهَ تَنَادَوْا، هَلُمُّوا إلَى حَاجَتِكُمْ. قَالَ: فَيَحُفُّونَهُمْ بِأجْنِحَتِهِمْ إلَى السَّمَاءِ الدُّنْيَا. قَالَ. فَيَسْألُهُمْ رَبُّهُمْ – وَهُوَ أعْلَمُ مِنْهُمْ: مَا يَقُولُ عِبَادِي؟ قَالَ: تَقُولُ: يُسَبِّحُونَكَ وَيُكَبِّرُونَكَ وَيَحْمَدُونَكَ وَيُمَجِّدُونَكَ. قَالَ فَيَقُولُ: هَلْ رَأوْنِي؟ قَالَ: فَيَقُولُونَ: لَا وَاللَّهِ مَا رَأوْكَ. قَالَ: فَيَقُولُ: وَكَيْفَ لَوْ رَأوْنِي؟ قَالَ: يَقُولُونَ: لَوْ رَأوْكَ كَانُوا أشَدَّ لَكَ عِبَادَةً، وَأشَدَّ لَكَ تَمْجِيدًا، وَأكْثَرَ لَكَ تَسْبِيحًا. قَالَ: يَقُولُ: فَمَا يَسْألُونَنِي؟ قَالَ: يَسْألُونَكَ الْجَنَّةَ. قَالَ: يَقُولُ: وَهَلْ رَأوْهَا؟ قَالَ: يَقُولُونَ: لَا وَاللَّهِ يَا رَبِّ! مَا رَأوْهَا. قَالَ: يَقُولُ: فَكَيْفَ لَوْ أنَّهُمْ رَأوْهَا؟ قَالَ: يَقُولُونَ: لَوْ أنَّهُمْ رَأوْهَا كَانُوا أشَدَّ عَلَيْهَا حِرْصًا، وَأشَدَّ لَهَا طَلَبًا، وَأعْظَمَ فِيهَا رَغْبَةً. قَالَ: فَمِمَّ يَتَعَوَّذُونَ؟ قَالَ: يَقُولُونَ: مِنْ النَّارِ. قَالَ: يَقُولُ: وَهَلْ رَأوْهَا؟ قَالَ: يَقُولُونَ: لَا وَاللَّهِ يَا رَبِّ! مَا رَأوْهَا. قَالَ: يَقُولُ: فَكَيْفَ لَوْ رَأوْهَا؟ قَالَ: يَقُولُونَ: لَوْ رَأوْهَا كَانُوا أشَدَّ مِنْهَا فِرَارًا، وَأشَدَّ لَهَا مَخَافَةً. قَالَ: فَيَقُولُ: فَأُشْهِدُكُمْ أنِّي قَدْ غَفَرْتُ لَهُمْ. قَالَ: يَقُولُ مَلَكٌ مِنَ الْمَلَائِكَةِ: فِيهِمْ فُلَانٌ، لَيْسَ مِنْهُمْ، إنَّمَا جَاءَ لِحَاجَةٍ. قَالَ: هُمْ الْجُلَسَاءُ لَا يَشْقَى بِهِمْ جَلِيسُهُمْ.

Abu Hurayrah ؓ *narrates that the Messenger of Allah* ﷺ *said:*

Allah has angels who wander around on roads in search of people who remember Allah. When they find such people they call other angels, "Come to your coveted company." Then they spread their wings over them up to the lowest Heaven. Their Lord asks them, although He knows better about them, "What are My servants saying?" They reply, "They are glorifying You, proclaiming Your Greatness, praising You and pronouncing Your Grandeur." The Messenger of Allah said, "Then Allah asks, 'Have they seen Me?' They reply, "No, by Allah, they have not seen You." The Messenger of Allah said, "Allah asks, 'How would have they acted, if they had seen Me?' They reply, 'Had they seen You, they would have worshipped You, magnified You and glorified You more earnestly.' Then Allah asks, 'What are they asking Me for?' The angels say, 'They are asking You for Paradise.' The Messenger of Allah said, "Allah asks, 'Have they seen it?' They reply, 'No, we swear by Allah, our Lord, they have not seen it.' He asks, 'How would have they acted if they had seen it?' The angels reply, 'If they had seen it, they would have been more intensely eager for it, would have asked more earnestly for it and would have had a greater desire for it.' He asks, 'What are they seeking refuge from?' They reply, 'From the Hell.' He asks, 'Have they seen it?' They reply, 'No, by our Lord, they have not seen this as well.' He asks, 'What would have been their state, had they seen it?' They reply, 'Had they seen it, they would have fled from it with greater speed and greater fear.' He says, 'Bear witness that I have forgiven them.' Some of the angels submit, 'Among them is so-and-so who has come for his own purpose (and not to join in remembrance).' Allah says, 'He has been in their company and those who join their company do not remain deprived.'" (Bukhari)

Say, *yaa Allah! Laa ilaaha illa-Llah*! *Allahumma ajirnaa min an-naar*, "O Allah! Save me from Hellfire." It is recommended to say this seven times a day in the morning, seeking refuge in Allah from Hellfire, asking Allah for Paradise, asking to see Him in *Akhirah*, asking Allah for everything. In the end He will say, "You are My Witness that I have forgiven them, so go and celebrate your happiness by making *Mawlid* for Prophet ﷺ." That is our celebration for happiness, not to entertain ourselves here and there. No, our happiness is in Muhammad ﷺ, our life is in Muhammad ﷺ, our love to our children and family is in Muhammad ﷺ, everything for us is Muhammad ﷺ, because he takes us to the door of Allah ﷻ!

One of the angels will say, "There is one between them who is not from them, he only came to see so-and-so. He didn't make *dhikr*, he only came to speak to someone."

Allah ﷻ will say, "Anyone who comes to sit even for a moment with those who are sitting for Allah's Love will be granted freedom from

Hellfire!" Allah will keep those friends together. A person may come for some other need, but because he is a friend of these circles of *dhikr*, Allah will forgive him.

O viewers! This is very little of what treasures of Islam you can find. Read about the greatness of *dhikrullah*, which has no limits of rewards, nor can anyone understand how much Allah will reward those who sit in *dhikr*, ladies and men, who ask from Him!

وَالذَّاكِرِينَ اللَّهَ كَثِيرًا وَالذَّاكِرَاتِ أَعَدَّ اللَّهُ لَهُم مَّغْفِرَةً وَأَجْرًا عَظِيمًا

Wa 'dh-dhaakireena 'Llaaha katheeran wa 'dh-dhaakiraati a`adda-Llaahu lahum maghfiratan wa ajran `azheema.

And men who remember Allah much and women who remember, for them has Allah prepared forgiveness and great reward. (Surat al-Ahzaab, 33:35)

One of the great scholars, al-Khawwas ؓ, said, "It is important for the one sitting in the *dhikr* association to make *dhikr* with complete force." It is like some people here, when you mention something they like to proclaim loudly, "*Takbeer! Allahu Akbar!*" That is how it should be said. Allah likes His Servants to call Him with love. If you say it softly you will be rewarded, but you have to show eagerness for love of Allah ﷻ and love of Prophet ﷺ. The scholar said, "He has to be with a group of people." Why does he have to be with a group of people and not alone? You can do it by yourself, but he insisted that you have to be with a group of people because of the following:

يد الله مع على الجماعة

Yadullaahi ma`a 'l-jama`ah.
The Hand of Allah is with the congregation. (Tirmidhi, Bukhari)

For this reason, it is preferable to say your prayers in *jama`ah* and to make *dhikr* in *jama`ah*, where veils are lifted up. By yourself you may not have the same eagerness to recite strongly so the veils will not be raised quickly, but in *jama`ah* Allah ﷻ will take them away. Allah has described our hearts as big stones. Can you break a large stone with a hammer? No. What do you need? You need a bulldozer and *jama`ah* is like a bulldozer! When someone says "Allah" by himself it is like a tractor, but with a *jama`ah* it is like a bulldozer, paving the way. A group of people with one hammer can break a stone, but one person with the same hammer cannot.

May Allah ﷻ make us break the stone of our hearts! He broke it for Sayyidina Musa ﷺ because he is *Kaleemullah.*

قَالَ رَبِّ أَرِنِي أَنظُرْ إِلَيْكَ قَالَ لَن تَرَانِي وَلَـكِنِ انظُرْ إِلَى الْجَبَلِ فَإِنِ اسْتَقَرَّ مَكَانَهُ فَسَوْفَ تَرَانِي فَلَمَّا تَجَلَّى رَبُّهُ لِلْجَبَلِ جَعَلَهُ دَكًّا وَخَرَّ موسَى صَعِقًا فَلَمَّا أَفَاقَ قَالَ سُبْحَانَكَ تُبْتُ إِلَيْكَ وَأَنَا أَوَّلُ الْمُؤْمِنِينَ

He said, "O my Lord! Show Yourself to me, that I may look upon You." Allah said, "By no means can you see Me (directly), but look upon the mountain; if it abides in its place, then you shall see Me." When his Lord manifested His glory on the mount, He made it as dust, and Moses fell down in a swoon. When he recovered his senses, he said, "Glory be to You! To You I return in repentance, and I am the first to believe." *(Surat al-`Araaf, 7:143)*

Sayyidina Musa ﷺ perceived no boundaries and he unknowingly crossed the limits by saying, "*Yaa Rabbee*! I want to see You!"

Allah ﷻ said, "You cannot see Me. How can you see Me on earth?"

Allah cannot be contained, everything is contained by Allah's power, but Allah has no place! You cannot say He is this or that, or He is up or down. Allah ﷻ has no place, no time, and no "where."

Sayyidina Musa ﷺ said, "Let me see You."

Allah said, "Okay, I love you and will tell you what you need to do. Look at the mountain and I will manifest My Beautiful Names and Attributes on it. If the mountain stays in its place, then you can see Me."

When Allah ﷻ manifested His Beautiful Names and Attributes, the mountain shattered to dust and Sayyidina Musa fainted, as the mountain was his ego! Allah ﷻ manifested His Beautiful Names and Attributes on the heart of Sayyidina Musa, what Sayyidina Muhiyuddeen ibn `Arabi ق said was the mountain of egoism that was broken. Sayyidina Musa ﷺ was in a coma, Allah destroyed his power, and made him know nothing. When he repented he stood up, when Allah wanted him to come back. Our mountains, our egos are so huge and arrogant, and we are so proud of ourselves, but we have to be soft and humble, and in order to be humble we must come to such associations to remember Allah ﷻ and His Prophet ﷺ, and Allah will remember you in a place better than this.

أنَا جَلِيْسُ مَنْ ذكَرَنِي

Ana jaleesu man dhakaranee.

I sit with him who remembers Me. *(Suyuti, Ahmad, Bayhaqi)*

Mention Allah daily and you will find Him whenever you are in need!

May Allah ﷻ forgive us and may Allah ﷻ bless us.

Wa min Allahi 't-tawfīq, bi ḥurmati 'l-ḥabīb, bi ḥurmati 'l-Fātiḥah.

And with Allah is success. For the sake of the Beloved, for his sake we recite the opening chapter of Holy Qur'an.

The Key to the Heavenly Dome of the White Pearl

A'ūdhu billāhi min ash-Shayṭāni 'r-rajīm. Bismillāhi' r-Raḥmāni 'r-Raḥīm. Nawaytu 'l-arbā'īn, nawaytu 'l-'itikāf, nawaytu'l-khalwah, nawaytu 'l-'uzlah, nawaytu 'r-riyāḍa, nawaytu 's-sulūk, lillāhi Ta'alā fi hādhā 'l-masjid. Atī'ūllāha wa atī'ū 'r-Rasūla wa ūlī 'l-amri minkum.
Obey Allah, obey the Prophet, and obey those in authority among you. (4:59)

Dastūr, madad yā Sulṭān al-Awlīyā, Mawlana Shaykh Nazim al-Haqqani ق.
Dastūr, madad yā Sulṭān al-Awlīyā, Mawlana Shaykh 'AbdAllah ad-Daghestani ق.

I came here tonight with happiness to see these young ones who are happy to be in a place where the name of the Prophet ﷺ is being mentioned! On the topic of, "The Jewel of Creation," all I am going to say is, *Muhammadun basharun wa laysakal bashari, Huwa yaqootatan wan-naasu ka 'l-hajari.* "Muhammad is a man, but not like any man. Muhammad is a diamond and all other human beings are pebbles." This is the answer to the topic, "The Jewel of Creation." In his *Burdah ash-Sharifah,* Imam Busayri ق said, *Muhammadun basharun,* "Although Sayyidina Muhammad ﷺ is a human being, he is unlike other humans."

What is the difference then? Today if you look at the news you will see a space shuttle landed on Mars. They say since it was launched, it travelled millions of miles for three-to-four years, and then landed on Mars and now the first pictures it took are coming. Do you think this is too much? This is nothing! The Prophet ﷺ went to *Qaaba Qawsayni aw Adnaa,* the Station of Two Bows' Length or Nearer, not just to Mars; he went beyond Mars and this Universe! He even went beyond what can exist; he reached nearness to Allah ﷻ of Two Bows' Length or less, and he didn't need anything in the way of transport to get there! They say the *Buraaq,* a heavenly steed, carried him, but really, who carried whom; did *Buraaq* carry the Prophet ﷺ or was the Prophet ﷺ carrying *Buraaq*? As soon as he sat on the *Buraaq,* he was carrying it! He carries everyone, so can he not carry *Buraaq*?

As it is mentioned by Muhiyuddeen Ibn al-Arabi ق, Allah ﷻ ordered Jibreel ﷺ to go get a *Buraaq* and descend to the Prophet ﷺ, and when he went to select it, he saw infinite numbers of *buraaqs,* not just one. All of them were the same shape, face and form that Allah ﷻ had created, there was no difference, and all of them were making *salawaat* on the Prophet ﷺ, because Allah ﷻ mentioned:

إِنَّ اللَّهَ وَمَلَائِكَتَهُ يُصَلُّونَ عَلَى النَّبِيِّ يَا أَيُّهَا الَّذِينَ آمَنُوا صَلُّوا عَلَيْهِ وَسَلِّمُوا تَسْلِيمًا

Inna-Llaaha wa malaa'ikatahu yusalloona `ala 'n-nabiyy, yaa ayyuha 'Lladheena aamanoo salloo `alayhi was sallimoo tasleema.

Verily, Allah and His angels send praise on the Prophet. O Believers! Pray upon him and greet him. *(Surat al-'Ahzaab, 33:56)*

They were all making *salawaat* on the Prophet ﷺ in one tune. They were making *dhikrullah,* because *salawaat* on Prophet ﷺ is also *dhikrullah.* So Jibreel ؑ looked around to see, which one to choose? He had to choose one. He looked at the last row; don't try to be in the first rows as that shows arrogance! Run to the back rows. Sometimes people complain, "They didn't respect me, they didn't give me a chair, they didn't make me their *imam.*" Why do you want to become an *imam* and carry all the people behind you; no need! Be sheep, not the shepherd! If you are the shepherd, you will have to look after all the sheep and never relax for a minute, but the sheep only graze and sleep, so let the shepherd do the work! Mawlana Shaykh Nazim ق is a good shepherd; he doesn't let his sheep fall in the valley where the hyenas eat them, and now there are too many hyenas all over the world!

So Sayyidina Jibreel ؑ looked in a corner and saw one of these *buraaqs* in a place in Paradise and it was crying, tears coming from its eyes. Shaykh Muhiyuddeen Ibn al-Arabi ق explains that from each of *Buraaq's* teardrops, pearls flowed! When *buraaqs* cry, pearls flow out, not as a drop but like rivers, and each pearl is bigger than this universe and is a paradise for a *mu'min,* the one who loves the Prophet ﷺ in this world!

Sayyidina Jibreel ؑ saw all those pearls coming from *Buraaq's* eyes and asked, "Why are you sad? Allah ﷻ made you angels and still you are sad?"

The *Buraaq* replied, "*Yaa* Jibreel ؑ! When Allah ﷻ created us all at the same time and ordered us to do *salawaat,* he mentioned the name of Prophet Muhammad ﷺ! Since then I felt love for him and was worried that some other *buraaq* besides me would carry him. I have been crying from my love for him and my longing to see him face-to-face, and I made *du'a, 'Yaa Rabbee*! Make me the one who carries Your Beloved ﷺ to You!' Since then I've had *ishq,* Iintense love for Prophet ﷺ: my food and my *dhikr* is to mention his name and my life is for the Prophet ﷺ! *Yaa* Jibreel ﵇, please take me!'"

So Jibreel ﵇ said, "You are the one I am taking!"

Buraaq ﵇ asked Sayyidina Jibreel ﵇ to choose him, and he was chosen! So what about human beings? The Prophet ﷺ is the Jewel of Creation in everyone's eyes, and that is the secret Allah ﷻ made when he went to *Israa'* and *Mi`raaj* without anything happening to him. Can you do that? How was he able to go and come back in the same form? He reached a place that Jibreel ﵇ could not pass, to the Divine Presence, *Qaaba Qawsayni aw Adna,* two bow lengths or less, perhaps two inches, one inch, one millimeter; no one knows but Allah ﷻ, and that secret will be open on the Day of Judgment. He is a jewel, the ruby, which is red, and Prophet's ﷺ face is pinkish red, his hair is black, reddish. He is a jewel and the rest of human beings are a pebble or rock. We can't compare ourselves to Prophet ﷺ, no one, not angels, not humans, whether some may like it or not. We are *Ahlu 's-Sunnah wa 'l-Jama`ah a*nd we love him!

"The ear has never heard and the eye has never seen." I will mention something about *salawaat,* that Allah gave to the Prophet ﷺ. According to Ibn Abbas ﵁, Allah ﷻ gave something to the *ummah* that is great. Not everything is building or skyscrapers; look at what that hadith says, "It's better than buildings or high rises, or better than the whole *dunya.*" And the Prophet ﷺ said:

> *Man qaala Bismillahi 'r-Rahmani 'r-Raheem katab allahu lahu bi kulli harfin arba`at alaaf hasanaat.*
>
> *For every letter of 'Bismillahi 'r-Rahmani 'r-Raheem' Allah will write for you four-thousand blessings.*

There are nineteen letters in *Bismillahi 'r-Rahmani 'r-Raheem* that, multiplied by four-thousand makes 76,000 *hasanaat* just for saying *"Bismillahi 'r-Rahmani 'r-Raheem"* one time! Moreover, *wa mahaa `anhu arba `alaaf sayi`aat,* Allah will take away four-thousand sins for each letter, which means 76,000 sins removed for one recitation of *"Bismillahi 'r-Rahmani 'r-Raheem,"* and *wa rafa..`alaa darajaat,* "He raised him four-thousand levels in Paradise." That means Allah ﷻ will raise you 76,000 levels when you say *"Bismillahi 'r-Rahmani 'r-Raheem."*

Allah ﷻ gave that to the Prophet ﷺ for the *ummah*! Can you get any richer? Say, *"Bismillahi 'r-Rahmani 'r-Raheem"* one-hundred times every day.

Multiply 76,000 by one-hundred, which is 7,600,000 *sayyi`aat* that Allah ﷻ takes from you and raises your levels in Paradise with only one-hundred *Bismillahi 'r-Rahmani 'r-Raheem*. So, are you going to read it or not?

It is said in the *tafseer* of the Holy Qur'an, ad-Durr al-Manthour from Imam Suyuti ؓ, which includes many *tafseer* and *ahadith*:

Allah created an angel under the Throne, whose head is like the head of human beings and he has 70,000 wings. On his right cheek is written the *Ayat al-Kursi* and on his left cheek is written, *"Shahid Allahu annahu laa ilaaha illa-Llah huw 'al....qaimam bil qist,"* and between his forehead (two eyes) *Surat al-Fatihah* is written, and between his two hands Allah ﷻ created 70,000 rows of angels and no one knows how long these rows are; there is no limit, an infinite number of angels are standing between his hands in 70,000 rows. They read the *Fatihah* from his forehead and when they say, *"Iyyaka na`budu wa iyyaka nasta`een. Yaa Rabbee,* we worship You and we ask help from You," then they go into *sajda,* and Allah ﷻ says to them, *"Arfa` ruoosakum,* raise your heads and I am happy with you," and all of them say, *"Yaa Rabbee,* please be happy with *Ummat al-Muhammad* ﷺ! Be happy with those people who love the Prophet ﷺ," and Allah ﷻ says, "You are My Witness that I am happy with them and forgive them."

We have already been forgiven! Just by reading *Surat al-Fatihah* one time, by the *barakah* and greatness of Sayyidina Muhammad ﷺ!

During *Mi`raaj,* the Prophet ﷺ saw a great white dome made from *durratum,* white pearl, the length of which was five-thousand heavenly years, which cannot be counted, similar to what Allah ﷻ said in the Holy Qur'an:

وَإِنَّ يَوْمًا عِندَ رَبِّكَ كَأَلْفِ سَنَةٍ مِّمَّا تَعُدُّونَ

Wa inna yawma inda rabbika ka-alfi sannatin mimma ta`udoon.

Verily a Day in the Sight of your Lord is like a thousand years of your reckoning. *(Surat-al Hajj, 22:47)*

The door and rocks of that dome were made of gold. If all the human beings and *jinn* that Allah ﷻ created sit on that dome, they would still be like a bird sitting on top of a mountain; the bird would look bigger and they would look smaller! So you cannot imagine. The Prophet ﷺ intended to enter it from the back side and not from the front.

A Voice said, *"Yaa Rasoolullah ﷺ!* Why don't you enter through the door?"

He said, "It is closed."

The Voice said, "Allah gave you the key, *yaa* Muhammad ﷺ! Use it and go inside."

The Prophet ﷺ said, "Where is the key?"

The Voice said, "Allah ﷻ gave you '*Bismillahi 'r-Rahmani 'r-Raheem*.'"

So the Prophet ﷺ recited, "*Bismillahi 'r-Rahmani 'r-Raheem*" and the door opened.

Whoever says "*Bismillahi 'r-Rahmani 'r-Raheem*" will enter that dome! Recite "*Bismillahi 'r-Rahmani 'r-Raheem*!" So now we said "*Bismillahi 'r-Rahmani 'r-Raheem*" and it is mentioned by the Prophet ﷺ in that story that we will be entering that dome one day *inshaa-Allah* and we hope it will be in *dunya* before *Akhirah*, and then in *Akhirah* also!

The Prophet ﷺ saw four rivers in it. from one of the rivers, there was such water flowing, that never changes! Always remains like crystal blue and fresh. That river was originating from the letter *meem* of *Bismillahi 'r-Rahmani 'r-Raheem*. There was like an opening in the letter *meem* and this water was gushing out of it! There is no description of that water! Another river was of milk, *laban*, coming out from the letter *ha* of Allah. From the *meem* of al-Raheem, a river of honey was coming out! Allah ﷻ said, " *Yaa* Muhammad ﷺ! Whoever has mentioned and made *dhikr* with these Names that I gave to your *ummah*, I will give them to drink from these four rivers!"

Those are the letters of *Bismillahi 'r-Rahmani 'r-Raheem*. Say "*Bismillahi 'r-Rahmani 'r-Raheem*." May Allah ﷻ give Sayyidina Muhammad ﷺ more greatness and more *`azhamah*, because when Allah ﷻ gives to the Prophet ﷺ, he gives to the *ummah* as he doesn't keep anything for himself: he is the one who gives everything and doesn't keep anything!

I heard from Grandshaykh ق that on the Day of Judgment, the Prophet ﷺ will make *sajda* in Allah's Divine Presence, and according to a *hadith* related by Imam Bukhari in the book Adab-al-Mufrat, he will make three *sajdas*. In each *sajda* Allah ﷻ will give him one third of the *ummah* to take to Paradise and after he makes three *sajdas*, he will also give everything that Allah ﷻ gave him as a reward and will dress the *ummah* with it. He will not keep anything for himself. He will go to Allah ﷻ and say, "*Yaa Rabbee!* I come to you with nothing! Whatever you want to do with me, You do!"

That is the Prophet ﷺ, the Jewel of Creation, whom Sayyidina Muhammad al-Busayri ق mentioned as: *Muhammadun basharun wa laysakal bashari, Huwa yaqootatan wan-naasu ka'l-hajari.* "Muhammad is a man, but not like any man. Muhammad is a diamond and all other human beings are pebbles."

May Allah ﷻ support you all and give you happiness in your life!

May Allah ﷻ forgive us and may Allah ﷻ bless us.

Wa min Allahi 't-tawfiq, bi ḥurmati 'l-ḥabīb, bi ḥurmati 'l-Fātiḥah.

And with Allah is success. For the sake of the Beloved, for his sake we recite the opening chapter of Holy Qur'an.

The Secrets of Alif and Ba

Aʿūdhu billāhi min ash-Shayṭāni 'r-rajīm. Bismillāhi' r-Raḥmāni 'r-Raḥīm.
Nawaytu 'l-arbāʿīn, nawaytu 'l-ʿitikāf, nawaytu'l-khalwah, nawaytu 'l-ʿuzlah,
nawaytu 'r-riyāḍa, nawaytu 's-sulūk, lillāhi Taʿalā fī hādhā 'l-masjid.
Atīʿūllāha wa atīʿū 'r-Rasūla wa ūlī 'l-amri minkum.
Obey Allah, obey the Prophet, and obey those in authority among you. (4:59)

Dastūr, madad yā Sulṭān al-Awlīyā, Mawlana Shaykh Nazim al-Haqqani ق.
Dastūr, madad yā Sulṭān al-Awlīyā, Mawlana Shaykh ʿAbdAllah ad-Daghestani ق.

First, good tidings for anyone who observed this night and who tried to observe this night, it is written that he observed *Laylat al-Qadr*. Mawlana Shaykh sent this message just now, and *inshaa-Allah,* Allah will write us amongst those who observed *Laylat al-Qadr*. He will share their *`ibaadah* with us since we are weak servants. And may Allah ﷻ unite our prayers with the worship of Sayyidina Muhammad ﷺ: his prayer, fasting, his *zakaat*, *Hajj* and his *Laylat al-Qadr*. *Bi hurmati 'l-habeeb, bi hurmati 'l-Fatihah.* Now anyone who wants to sleep can snore (no worry about this)!

So where did we arrive? We must always seek refuge in Allah ﷻ from Shaytan *ar-rajeem,* the one whom Allah cursed to be the lowest in Hellfire. *Ar-rajeem* is the one who is stoned by Allah ﷻ and by every person who goes to Hajj or who says, *"astaghfirullah."* That *istighfaar* is like a stone falling on the head of Shaytan!

Now in technology we have what they call "smart bombs," which they fire from here and can reach Yemen or China, to hit a high-precision target. To anyone who says *"astaghfirullah,"* the secret of *istighfaar* is that Allah creates a stone from that and shoots it like a smart bomb on *Iblees*'s head! So imagine how many people within 24 hours are saying *"astaghfirullah."* Every prayer is endless in how many times we make *istighfaar*. For example, if the prayer takes ten minutes and we breathe as *awliyaullah* say, 24,000 breaths, times 1.5 billion Muslims praying five times a day, that is six-billion times 24,000! You cannot count the number of stones going on Shaytan and his followers.

To say, *astaghfirullah al-`azheem wa atoobu ilayh,* "I repent to Allah the Greatest and I turn to Him," three times is the proper way to read after every prayer. *Tawbatan `abdan zhaaliman li nafsihi, laa yamliku li nafsihi hayaatan wa laa mawtan wa laa nushoora,* "repentance of a servant who is an oppressor to himself, who doesn't hold the power of life for himself, nor death, nor of resurrection," we are expressing our weakness and helplessness in front of Allah! The biggest weakness of human beings that we must use every day is our need to sleep; Allah ﷻ made us need sleep to show us that we are weak and helpless. If you don't sleep you have no power. *Awliyaullah* say that if you resist sleep for forty days, then whenever you get sleepy take fresh wudu, pray two raka`ats, freshen up, then for the rest of your life you will be able to overcome the need to sleep. May Allah ﷻ give us from their barakah!

Sleeping is what shows our weakness most; it shows that if you don't raise your head, you cannot survive. So don't say, "I don't need to sleep." Allah made *nu`aas,* drowsiness, come on everyone. There is *barakah* in sleeping, because when you sleep your inner tyrant stops and we are all tyrants against ourselves. That is why if you make *wudu*, pray two *raka`ats* and then sleep it is *`ibaadah* until you wake up, but if you sleep for eight hours without *wudu*, not one second of that eight hours will be written for you as *`ibaadah*!

May Allah ﷻ make it easy for us to make *wudu* and sleep. People sleep twelve hours, sometimes sixteen hours or two shifts of sleep. So when you say, *"A`oodhu billahi min ash-Shaytaani 'r-rajeem,"* it means you are seeking absolute refuge in Allah, and then everything after you say that word is forgiven and you are clean to enter the Ocean of *Bismillahi 'r-Rahmani 'r-Raheem.*

In the alphabet, *"Alif"* comes first and *"Ba"* comes second, is it not? *Alif* is always standing, like a pine tree that survives in summer and winter weather. *Alif* is always the first letter of "Allah," always *shamikha,* standing tall, straight, aloft. *Al-jibaal ash-shamikhaat* "the mountains are proud of their height," and *Alif* is proud of its station standing, and *kibriya,* pride, is only for Allah ﷻ. *Alif* is proud as it is the first letter in the Arabic language and without the first letter you cannot speak or your language might be wrong. Standing represents pride and arrogance. Allah has *kibriya,* pride, that says, "I am the King of Kings! In front of Me, no one can say he is a king!"

يَوْمَ هُم بَارِزُونَ لَا يَخْفَى عَلَى اللَّهِ مِنْهُمْ شَيْءٌ لِّمَنِ الْمُلْكُ الْيَوْمَ لِلَّهِ الْوَاحِدِ الْقَهَّارِ

The Day whereon they will (all) come forth; not a single thing concerning them is hidden from Allah. Whose will be the dominion that Day? That of Allah, the One, the Irresistible! *(Surat al-Ghaafir, 40:16)*

He calls Himself by Himself. When He orders Sayyidina Israfeel ﷺ to blow the trumpet, everyone will die, including him, Sayyidina Azra`eel ﷺ, and Sayyidina Jibreel ﷺ. Sayyidina Azra`eel said, "If I knew the pain that a *mu'min* goes through when he is dying, I would be soft with him." *Alhamdulillah,* the Prophet ﷺ said, "The soul of a *mu'min* comes out like a hair from ghee," which means without resistance and it comes out easily. Allah ﷻ is showed Sayyidina Azra`eel that there is pain, but in reality there is also *noor* there.

Grandshaykh ق related that when a *mu'min* leaves *dunya,* Allah orders Sayyidina Azra`eel to bring a heavenly paper with "Allah" written on it. When the *`abd* sees that paper, he will run after it and then his soul will come out of the body and enter the Ocean of *Qudrah* back to its origin, from where you were created.

إنّا لله و إنّا إليه راجعون

To Allah we belong and unto Him we return. *(Surat al-Baqara, 2:156)*

So *"Alif"* is always showing greatness and *"Ba"* is always showing humbleness by laying in *sajda* in front of *Alif.* That is why in European languages, *Alif,* represented by the letter "a," is first in the alphabet. Keep in mind that their *Alif,* the "a," shows *shirk* compared to the Arabic *Alif.* "A" is symbolized by three parts: one leg, a second leg and one in the middle. Allah ﷻ is telling them, "Don't let there be three, as Allah is One! Go back to the language of *Ahlu' l-Jannah,"* because *Alif* is one!

So the *Ba* is in *sajda* in front of *Alif,* but in *"Bismillahi 'r-Rahmani 'r-Raheem"* the *Ba* comes first. When you say, "In the Name of Allah," *bi Ismillah,* that preceeds your actions. It is spelled *Ba, Alif, Seen, Meem, "bi ism,"* so the *Alif* cannot be after *Ba,* which is why *huzifati 'l-Alif,* it is removed, and the *Ba* is then connected directly with the letter *Seen,* to become *"bismillah."* Out of respect, the *Ba* should not be before the *Alif,* so the language removed it from the sequence in the word *"b'ism,"* so the *Alif"* is gone.

Bismillahi 'r-Rahmani 'r-Raheem. This is how everything came out, through the *Ba:*

كنت كنزا مخفياً فأحببت أن أعرف فخلقت الخلق فبه عرفوني

Kuntu kanzan makhfiyyan fa ahbabtuhu an u`rafa fa khalaqtu 'l-khalq fa-bihi `arifoonee.

I was a Hidden Treasure (and) I wanted to be known, so I created Creation, and by it they knew Me. *(Hadith Qudsi)*

Fa "bi-hi" `arifoonee, "By *Ba* they knew Me." Who is the *Ba?* It is *al-Insaan al-Kaamil,* the Perfect Human Being, Sayyidina Muhammad ﷺ! *Awliyaullah* say Sayyidina Muhammad ﷺ is the Mirror through which *al-Khalq,* The Creator, can be seen. When Allah ﷻ wants to see Himself by Himself, with His Power, He looks in the Mirror, which is Sayyidina Muhammad ﷺ, and He sees the *khalq* there. The reality of *"Alastu bi-rabbikum"* on the Day of Promises is still there and has never changed, and what we see here is the reflection of what comes out of the Mirror that is Sayyidina Muhammad ﷺ. That is why Imam Ghazali ق said, *Mootoo qabla an tamootoo,* "Die (in ego) before you (physically) die." When your ego dies, you wake up and can then see the Reality! When your self is dead, Allah ﷻ opens your vision and you can see, because you will no longer show-off or be proud when you are in complete submission, and you will not run after *dunya;* rather, you will still be running after Allah ﷻ.

So the *wujood il-`aalim bi 'l-ba,* the reality of knowledge is in the *Ba,* because it is *fa bi-hi `arifoonee,* "through Me they knew Me." And looking at the *"bi"*we see the *Ba* is still the first letter. What is the proof that the *Ba* is the letter that describes our recognition and *tawheed*? What is the first letter that human beings mentioned on their tongues? *"Ba,"* when Allah ﷻ said to the souls, *"Alastu bi-rabbikum?"* and we said, "Yes, *balaa."* (*Surat al-A`raaf,,* 7:172)

So the first letter mentioned is the *Ba* and the Prophet ﷺ mentioned it in response to Allah ﷻ, everyone else followed him. So say, *"Ba,"* and say *"Alif."* When you mention *Alif,* what happens at the end? You close your lips. When you say *"Ba"* you open your lips. *Alif* is hidden, just as treasures are hidden. When you say *"Alif,"* you want to open the treasures but they remain closed, but when you say *"Ba,"* the knowledge is opened and all the *ma`arif* enter. No one can know Allah's ﷻ Greatness, so you cannot get it by saying *"Alif."* When He said, *"Alastu bi-rabbikum,"* they could not say "Allah," they said, *"Balaa,"* referring to Prophet ﷺ. When Sayyidina Muhammad ﷺ said, *"Ba,"* everyone said, *"Ba,"* and *`Uloomi 'l-Awwaleen wa 'l-Akhireen,* the Knowledge of the Firsts and Knowledge of the Lasts entered the body because you opened the place where provisions come in. Can you take in provision other than through your mouth? So when you open your mouth you receive and when you close your mouth you don't receive.

So, on the Day of Promises the Prophet ﷺ said, *"Balaa."* And when you say, *"Laa,"* you open your mouth. Now say, *"Yaa,"* because that is a *yaa* without dots; it is *Alif maqsoora,* half *Alif,* and again you are opening your mouth. So *"Balaa"* is written with three open letters, which means, *"Yaa Rabbee,* we are ready to receive!" May Allah ﷻ give us understanding. What is happening is the opening of our selves that were in the *`Alam adh-Dharr,* the World of Atoms, where we were the smallest in the smallest possible world that can be imagined, in the Presence of Allah ﷻ. How small? What size, no one knows. Allah will open the knowledge but only to His Prophet ﷺ, not to anyone else.

"Ba" is the first letter to be pronounced in Creation, because Prophet ﷺ was the first to say, "Yes." The first time was when Allah created Prophet's Light before creating the Creation and asked him, "Am I not your Lord?" other than when Allah asked everyone else. Prophet ﷺ said, "Yes." That is when Allah ﷻ raised Prophet's name up with His, as he is *al-Muwahhid wa 'l-Musaddiq bi Rabbihi `azza wa jal,* the one whose *tawheed* is perfect, who believes one-hundred percent with no doubt in his Creator!

Sayyidina Abu Bakr as-Siddiq ؓ got his title, *"as-Siddiq"* because he accepted whatever Prophet ﷺ said. Also, Prophet ﷺ was given his title because whatever Allah ﷻ showed him when he was Light, he accepted. You are not a Muslim only by saying, *"Laa ilaaha illa-Llah;"* you have to also say, *"Muhammadun Rasoolullah."*

Al-Ba showed a broken heart. When you are in front of a lover whom you love so much, and you know his greatness, you are always broken-hearted because you continuously seek more openings. Prophet ﷺ, the *Ba,* always wants more to open, which is why Allah ﷻ said:

أنا عند المنكسرة قلوبهم

I am with those whose hearts are broken for My sake.

(Hadith Qudsi, At-Haf 6/290)

"I am with the broken-hearted ones as they are always calling on Me." Also, *Ba* is always in *sajda* to *Alif,* to Allah ﷻ, which means the Prophet ﷺ is always in the position of *inkisaar,* brokenness, and showing humbleness. Allah is with the broken-hearted. Who has the most broken heart for the Love of his Lord? Prophet ﷺ! All his life and in *Akhirah,* it is Sayyidina Muhammad ﷺ who is always in the Presence of Allah ﷻ.

From its specialties, the *Ba* shows *tawaad`a,* humility, and a broken heart to Allah ﷻ. When they tried to put the dots (*nukta*) on *Ba,* every letter wanted the dot to be on top except *Ba,* who wanted the dot on the bottom, as if to say, "*Yaa Rabbee,* I don't want to be proud that the dot is on top of me because the center of the dot is the center of the heart, so I want it to be below," not above like in the letters *Taa, Thaa, Khaa, Jeem* in which the dot is in the middle. The *Ba* did not accept more than one dot, to show, "I submit completely, *yaa* Allah!"

The dot is the center of power, so it is carrying the *Ba*; were it on top it would push it down, but on the bottom it supports the *Ba.* Also, *Ba* has only one dot, which indicates, "I don't accept to love anyone else, *yaa Rabbee*! I have one *mahboob,* one love, not two, not three."

In order to understand the Beautiful Name "Allah," which encompasses all of Allah's Beautiful Names and Attributes, we must understand it can only be known through prayers and *du`a*:

دَعَوُا اللَّهَ مُخْلِصِينَ لَهُ الدِّينَ

Da`awoo Allaaha mukhliseena lahu 'd-deen.

They call to Allah, offering Him sincere devotion. *(Surat Luqman, 31:32)*

Fadullah, "ask Allah," but on the condition that you must be *mukhlis,* sincere, for your *du`a* to be accepted. If you say *fadullah wa lahu 'd-deen,* removing the word "*mukhlis,*" it has no more meaning. So if you are not sincere and you need a *du`a,* go to someone who is sincere and ask them to pray on your behalf for Allah ﷻ to accept what you want. This is why people go to *awliyaullah,* to get a *du`a* that will be accepted. I see many people, especially Pakistanis, say, "*Sawee du`a,*" as even in Arab countries they know *du`a* has to be through a pious person. "*Sawee du`a* for me." They believe your *du`a* is accepted. So if you want your *du`a* to be accepted, be *mukhlis,* then "*fadullah,*" call upon Allah, use that Name "Allah" in your *du`a,* as His Greatest Name is embedded in it.

May Allah ﷻ forgive us and may Allah ﷻ bless us.

Wa min Allahi 't-tawfiq, bi ḥurmati 'l-ḥabīb, bi ḥurmati 'l-Fātiḥah.

And with Allah is success. For the sake of the Beloved, for his sake we recite the opening chapter of Holy Qur'an.

All Creation is within Muhammad

A'ūdhu billāhi min ash-Shayṭāni 'r-rajīm. Bismillāhi' r-Raḥmāni 'r-Raḥīm.
Nawaytu 'l-arbā'īn, nawaytu 'l-'itikāf, nawaytu'l-khalwah, nawaytu 'l-'uzlah,
nawaytu 'r-riyāḍa, nawaytu 's-sulūk, lillāhi Ta'alā fi hādhā 'l-masjid.
Atī'ūllāha wa atī'ū 'r-Rasūla wa ūlī 'l-amri minkum.
Obey Allah, obey the Prophet, and obey those in authority among you. (4:59)

Dastūr, madad yā Sulṭān al-Awlīyā, Mawlana Shaykh Nazim al-Haqqani ق.
Dastūr, madad yā Sulṭān al-Awlīyā, Mawlana Shaykh 'AbdAllah ad-Daghestani ق.

We said previously the secret of the letter '*Ba*' with the dot under it, is that it shows the Door; the *Ba* is the Door to Allah ﷻ! The dot under the *Ba* is the whole Creation, because it begins with the first letter of the Holy Qur'an and the Holy Qur'an is Allah's Ancient Words, that are not created. *Bismillahi 'r-Rahmaani 'r-Raheem* is one *ayah* of Holy Qur'an, which means it is Divine, not created.

Therefore, *Ba* is a letter that is not created. The reality behind it is that Allah ﷻ put the reality of the Prophet ﷺ in it, which is why the *Ba* is always in *sajda* to the *Alif.* Its dot represents the *`Alam al-`Ulwiyya wa 'l-`Alam as-Sufliyya,* the Heavenly World and the Lower World. Out of respect to the Prophet ﷺ, who is always in *sajda,* the dot didn't accept to be on top, it stayed at the bottom.

The *Ba* symbolizes the reality of Sayyidina Muhammad ﷺ. Allah ﷻ began the Holy Qur'an with it and gave honor to the Prophet ﷺ. This is one of the meanings of:

وَرَفَعْنَا لَكَ ذِكْرَكَ

Wa rafa`naa laka dhikrak.

(O Muhammad!) We have raised your remembrance. (Surat ash-Sharh, 94:4)

This is because of the reality that Allah ﷻ has given to the Prophet ﷺ in the verse, "*Bismillahi 'r-Rahmaani 'r-Raheem.*" The Prophet ﷺ tells us that when Allah ﷻ revealed that verse to him on the Day of Promises, it was not only revealed to him when Jibreel ﷺ brought the Holy Qur'an, but when he said, "I was given *`Uloom al-Awwaleen wa 'l-Akhireen,* Knowledge of Before is Knowledge concerned with Heavenly Matters." Since the "*ba*" came at the beginning of the Holy Qur'an, it means the Prophet ﷺ was the first one to be created, as he said:

كنت نبيا وآدم بين الروح والجسد

Kuntu Nabiyyan wa Adamu bayni 'r-roohi wa 'l-jasad.

I was a Prophet while Adam was still between the spirit and the body.

(Tirmidhi)

This indicates that the Prophet ﷺ was before the creation of Adam, and when Allah ﷻ, according to the *hadith* of Prophet ﷺ (of Jaabir):

اول ما خلق الله نور نبيك يا جابر

Awwala maa khalaq-Allahu noora nabiyyika ya Jaabir!

The first thing Allah ﷻ created is the Light of the Prophet ﷺ.

And from that Light, He created Creation. And that Light of the Prophet ﷺ is always in *sajda* to Allah ﷻ, in that *"ba,"* the origin of that reality is from that *Noor,* that *"ba"* represents the *Noor* that was given to the Prophet ﷺ. Where Allah said:

لما أردت أن أخلق الخلق قبضت قبضة من نوري ، فقلت لها : كوني محمداً

Lamaa aaradtu an akhluq al-khalq qabadtu qabdatan min nooree fa-qultu lahu koonee Muhammada!

I grasped one handful from My Light and said to it, "Be, Muhammad!"

(Hadith Qudsi)

When He says "handful," it means like taking a handful of water from a river or an ocean, which is very little, and it means the remaining has no beginning and no end. And that Light began to shine, and it is from the Divine Attribute *"an-Noor."* So when Allah said, "I grasped a handful of Light from My Light," it means that Light's Source is Divine. And Allah ﷻ said, *"Koonee Muhammada!"* so Muhammad ﷺ has a Divine origin, and "Muhammad" is one of the Names Allah ﷻ has given to Creation: *kaana tahtahu kullu makhlookaat,* "Under him is all Creation." So if that Light was not Divine, he could not be with or among everyone, shining and attracting. It would not be possible for his name to be raised up with Allah's Name, of course not, because *Allah laa shareek lahu*. That means Allah gave Prophet ﷺ *fee hadd al-makhlooqaat,* within the limits of Creation, He made all the

Creation within the Prophet ﷺ. *Laa ilaaha illa-Llah Muhammadun Rasoolullah.* "*Muhammadun Rasoolullah*" represents Creation. The dot represents Creation, and what is in the dot we have not seen yet, but what we saw is a drop that represents an ocean.

Grandshaykh, may Allah bless his soul, said that when Allah ﷻ created the Light of the Prophet ﷺ, He put within it that Divine Light, that Reality, and that is why we say:

وَاعْلَمُوا أَنَّ فِيكُمْ رَسُولَ اللَّهِ

W `alamoo anna feekum Rasoolullah.

Know that Prophet is among you. *(Surat al Hujurat, 49:7)*

That is how they translate it, that means he is within you, not "among you." That means the Prophet ﷺ is very near to all of you at the same time, and no one can do that if he does not have a Divine Origin!

Either in Paradise or in death you will understand the Reality of the Prophet ﷺ, but in *dunya* no one can truly understand the Reality of the Prophet ﷺ, not even *Sahaabah* or the angels. How can you understand what is high? The one who is higher can see below, but how can the one who is down see high? So whatever they saw of the Reality of the Prophet ﷺ is still a drop of an ocean, and the Reality of Prophet ﷺ is a drop of the ocean of *an-Noor.*

So Grandshaykh ق said, as mentioned in the *hadith,* that Allah ﷻ put the Reality of the Prophet, that *Noor,* in *Bahr al-Qudrah,* and he was turning, and Allah ﷻ put the Reality of the Prophet ﷺ in a *misbaah,* lamp, *ka-annahaa kawkabun durriyy,* like a star of pearl.

اللَّهُ نُورُ السَّمَاوَاتِ وَالْأَرْضِ مَثَلُ نُورِهِ كَمِشْكَاةٍ فِيهَا مِصْبَاحٌ الْمِصْبَاحُ فِي زُجَاجَةٍ الزُّجَاجَةُ كَأَنَّهَا كَوْكَبٌ دُرِّيٌّ

Allahu nooru's-samawaati wa'l-ard. Mathalu noorihi ka-mishkaatin feehaa misbaahun al-misbaahu fee zujaajatin az-zujaajatu ka-annahaa kawkabun durriyy.

Allah is the Light of the Heavens and the Earth. The parable of His Light is as if there were a niche and within it a lamp: the lamp is in a glass, the glass like a Brilliant Star. *(Surat an-Noor, 24:35)*

The example of His Light, which is not His Light but lower than it--His Light is the Light of Heavens and Earth--but the example is what Prophet ﷺ is carrying of Allah's Light. *Mathala noorihi, ka-mishkaatin feehaa misbaah,* the example of His Light is like a bundle of different *masaabeeh,* lamps, on that bundle, and in the middle there is a Lamp, and that Lamp is like a universe of pearl. Why did He say "pearl?" To show the greatness of the Prophet ﷺ that is, *ka-annahaa kawkabun durriyy. Misbaah* we know. If you say, "I have a *misbaah,*" that is a lamp or lantern, and it is limited or small. But He said, "No, he is like a universe of *Noor,* Light." It means that *misbaah* which is small in your eyes is huge in Allah's Eyes, so Allah described him as *"kawkab,"* a universe within, which is all *makhlooqaat*! And the Light is coming from:

يُوقَدُ مِن شَجَرَةٍ مُّبَارَكَةٍ زَيْتُونَةٍ لَّا شَرْقِيَّةٍ وَلَا غَرْبِيَّةٍ يَكَادُ زَيْتُهَا يُضِيءُ وَلَوْ لَمْ تَمْسَسْهُ نَارٌ نُّورٌ عَلَى نُورٍ

Yuqadu min shajaratin mubaarakatin zaytoonatin laa sharqeeyyatin wa laa gharbeeyatin ya kaadu zaytuhaa yudee`u wa law lam tamssahu naarun noor `alaa noor.

Lit from a blessed tree, an olive tree that is neither of the East nor of the West, the oil of which is so bright that it would certainly give light of itself.

(Surat an-Noor, 4:35)

"From the oil of an olive tree, not Eastern nor Western," and that is something else we won't go into now. But as Grandshaykh ق said, Allah ﷻ put that Light inside the *misbaah,* which is the universe and the whole Creation that Allah ﷻ created. That is why it is revealed to *awliyaullah* that the Prophet ﷺ is a Prophet for every Creation!

Khidr ؑ asked Jibreel ؑ, "When did Allah create Sayyidina Adam?"

Jibreel ؑ replied, "Which Adam?"

He said, "Oh! Is there another Sayyidina Adam ؑ?"

Jibreel ؑ said, "You didn't see anything! He is the last Adam. There are 124,000 Adams that came and they have been judged, and those who are good are in Paradise, whereas those who are not have been sent to punishment, and the Prophet ﷺ is the Prophet to all of them."

Not the others; that is exclusively for Prophet Muhammad ﷺ as he represents the whole Creation, and in every moment there is a creation coming and a creation going! That's why in the *tafseer* of *Maaliki Yawmi 'd-*

deen, "The Owner of the Day of Judgment," the question is, "Which Day of Judgment?" Allah is "*al-Khaaliq*," and that means He is continuously creating, non-stop! So creations come and creations go; there might be ten creations coming and a hundred going, or a hundred coming and a hundred going in one moment! And for all of them the Prophet is present at the Judgment, as in the Divine Words of the Holy Qur'an:

فَمَن يَعْمَلْ مِثْقَالَ ذَرَّةٍ خَيْرًا يَرَهُ وَمَن يَعْمَلْ مِثْقَالَ ذَرَّةٍ شَرًّا يَرَهُ

Whosoever has done an atom's weight of good shall see it, and whosoever has done an atom's weight of evil shall see it. (Surah az-Zalzalah, 99:7-8)

And every nation is judged according to their `*amal*, and Prophet is the one who intercedes, *wa lahu ash-shafa`a*. The meaning of "*shafa`a*" is continuous, it doesn't stop, it is Divine. So he said that Light was under Allah's observation, which is *Bahr al-Qudrah*, as mentioned in the *hadith* of Jaabir, and that Light was turning in the *Bahr al-Qudrah*, and in Grandshaykh's ق interpretation, under that observation in that manifestation of what Allah manifested on Prophet , (we don't know what that is), for 70,000 years sending His *Tajalli* on Prophet , dressing him with heavenly, divine dresses that Allah wants him to be dressed by Allah's Order.

And Allah is dressing him directly, sending these *tajalliyaat* on the Reality of the Prophet , and Prophet began to sweat and that condensation began to appear from the warmth of those great manifestations. Sayyidina Musa fainted when Allah manifest His Beautiful Names on him, whereas the Prophet is a mountain! The mountain shattered for Sayyidina Musa , but the mountain for Sayyidina Muhammad stood:

لَوْ أَنزَلْنَا هَذَا الْقُرْآنَ عَلَى جَبَلٍ لَّرَأَيْتَهُ خَاشِعًا مُّتَصَدِّعًا مِّنْ خَشْيَةِ اللَّهِ وَتِلْكَ الْأَمْثَالُ نَضْرِبُهَا لِلنَّاسِ لَعَلَّهُمْ يَتَفَكَّرُونَ

Had We sent down this Qur'an on a mountain, verily, thou wouldst have seen it humble itself and cleave asunder for fear of Allah. Such are the similitudes which We propound to men, that they may reflect. (Surat al-Hashr, 59:21)

For Sayyidina Musa , the mountain shattered to dust and he fainted when that *tajalli* came, but the Prophet did not. So then Allah created

Prophets from that sacred condensation, and they are still inside the Lamp feeling that warmth, shyness, and annihilation, that they are nothing in that Absolute Power that Allah ﷻ is giving and revealing to Prophet ﷺ! And he began to feel he cannot raise his head and all these emotions came out, and he thought, "Did I deserve that?" Allah is sending, sending, He is the *Akram al-Akrameen*, the Most Generous of All Generous Ones. No one can be called *"al-Kareem,"* and if you do you are committing a sin, as (properly) it is *"`Abdul-Kareem,"* servant of Kareem.

More condensation came and those drops are the *awliyaullah.* Then more condensation came and the rest of Creation began to appear. All of their realities are within the Lamp; were they outside of it the universe could not carry them because in the Lamp they are clean and if they come out of the reality of cleanliness to dirtiness, this universe would shatter. But only a reflection of their reality is shining out of the Lamp. They are reflections of the reality, which is how they appear in *dunya*. Everyone that appears exists, but their real existence is there. Here in *dunya* they are a reflection, so that's why Allah destroys that image because it is not real. That means that mirror is taken away from you and that reality can no longer transmit or reflect through it to appear in *dunya.*

That is why Allah ﷻ said everything is created *'zawjayn.'*

وَمِن كُلِّ شَيْءٍ خَلَقْنَا زَوْجَيْنِ لَعَلَّكُمْ تَذَكَّرُونَ

Wa min kulli shayin khalaqnaa zawjayn la`allakum tadhakkaroon.

And of all things We have created pairs; perhaps you will remember.

(Surat adh-Dhaariyat, 51:49)

"From everything We have created two." Allah didn't say, "from human beings;" He mentioned human beings elsewhere, that Allah created Sayyidina Adam ؑ and from him He created Hawwa ؑ, but that is different. Here He said, *wa min kulli shayin,* He created two of "everything." Everything! Allah created two: the real and the image. The real is still in the Lamp as *dunya* cannot carry it.

That is why Grandshaykh ق said that when the Prophet ﷺ entered *Qaaba Qawsayni aw Adnaa,* Allah ﷻ dressed him and Sayyidina Jibreel ؑ said to the Prophet ﷺ, "I cannot continue! Go." How can *dunya* carry that heavenly *tajalli*? So Grandshaykh ق said that the Reality of Prophet ﷺ stayed in *Qaaba Qawsayni aw Adnaa,* and only one ray of it came back from that station, because had he returned in that full state *dunya* would have shattered!

So our Reality is there, and from everything Allah created two: the reality and an image that you see here. Allah gave this image a time in which to appear, similar to what scientists discovered in the after-glow of stars that have been dead [reaching us from] many light years. So when your reflection goes to the mirror of Reality, the light is reflected in the mirror of the lamp and you appear, and when the order comes to shut that mirror you disappear. Then you are dead as the soul is gone.

All that was given to the Prophet ﷺ and that is why when Jibreel ؑ said to the Prophet ﷺ *"Iqraa!"* he said, *maa anaa bi qaaree*? "What am I going to read?"[2] Jibreel ؑ said, "Read *'Bismi.'*" So the first letter of the Holy Qur'an was *"Ba,"* which represents Prophet ﷺ, meaning, *"Yaa* Muhammad! We opened that and gave it to you."

When Jibreel ؑ said, *"Bismi,"* if you continue the *ayah*:

اقرَأ باسْمِ رَبِّكَ الَّذِي خَلَقَ

Iqraa bismi Rabbika 'Lladhee khalaq.

Read! In the Name of your Lord Who created. *(Surat al-`Alaq, 96:1-2)*

So He wants to give him the permission to see the Creation, because think about it, how do you read? It means he is seeing what he is reading, is it not? When someone says to you, *Iqraa*! "Read!" you see what you read. So when you read "In the Name of Allah," then Allah shows you what He created: *Iqraa bismi Rabbika 'Lladhee khalaq*. So the Reality of the Prophet ﷺ and of Creation is in the Lamp.

So when Adam disappears with his children, this whole group will no longer be reflected as they have gone back to their origin and they stay there. So that is why Allah ﷻ addressed them when they were inside the Lamp in the Presence of the Prophet ﷺ; they cannot be in the Presence of Allah ﷻ, they are in the Presence of the Prophet ﷺ and the Prophet ﷺ is in the Presence of His Lord! And so, He said to them, "Am I not your Lord?"

---

[2] Most commentators consider the meaning of *"maa anaa bi qaree"* to be "I am not a reader," but it has also been transmitted as, "What shall I read?"

and the first answer was *"Balaa,"* the first letter was the *"ba,"* they opened their mouth, their lips moved. You open your mouth when you are in a good mood, and you see something extraordinary you say, "ooh!" and when you see something that is not nice in front of you, you also open your mouth, so opening the mouth is a characteristic that Allah gave to let you receive the knowledge of the *"ba."* And after the *"ba"* He mentioned three more of Allah's Beautiful Names and Attributes. What are they? Allah, *ar-Rahman* and *ar-Raheem*.

So Allah ﷻ, as scholars say, has three-thousand Names:

ذَلِكَ مَبْلَغُهُم مِّنَ الْعِلْمِ

That is as far as knowledge will reach them. *(Surat an-Najm, 53:30)*

But really it is an infinite number of Names. When you appear in *dunya* your existence has to be under one of Allah's Beautiful Names and Attributes or else you cannot appear, so you appear with a Divine Name. Allah ﷻ has infinite Names and Attributes, but what we know, as they say, there are three-thousand Names, of which: one-thousand He revealed to the angels; one-thousand He revealed to the Prophets; three-hundred each are in the *Zaboor* (Psalms), *Tawraat*, (Old Testament), and *Injeel* (New Testament), which totals 900; and, there are Ninety-Nine Names in the Holy Qur'an, and Allah kept One Name known only to Himself, which is *Ismullah al-`Azham*!

إِنَّ اللَّهَ وَمَلَائِكَتَهُ يُصَلُّونَ عَلَى النَّبِيِّ يَا أَيُّهَا الَّذِينَ آمَنُوا صَلُّوا عَلَيْهِ وَسَلِّمُوا تَسْلِيمًا

Verily, Allah and His angels send praise on the Prophet. O Believers! Pray upon him and greet him with all respect. *(Surat al-Ahzaab, 33:56)*

From the one-thousand Names that Allah ﷻ revealed to the angels that make *tasbeeh* (as noted in the verse above), it means Allah and His Angels are making *salawaat* on the Prophet ﷺ and dressing him with those one-thousand Names. Of the one-thousand Names that Allah revealed to the Prophets, it means they were given to the Prophet ﷺ. The nine-hundred Names are contained in the Holy Books of Allah, and since the Holy Qur'an wrapped them all, and including the ninety-nine Names in the Qur'an, those are a summary. That is why, *Yaseen qalb ul-Qur'an, "Surat al-Yaseen* is the heart of the Qur'an." So the Prophet ﷺ, whose name is *"Yaseen,"* is the heart of the Qur'an and the Holy Qur'an is the heart of all books, and *Surat al-Fatihah* is the heart of *Yaseen*, and *Ismullah al-`Azham* is the reality of *Yaseen*!

But what is *Ismullah al-`Azham*? We cannot go into this subject as it is above our level, and then people might criticize, so no need to discuss it here. There is one Name left, which Allah kept for Himself. Scholars say when you read, "*Bismillahi 'r-Rahmani 'r-Raheem,*" you are reading the Name of *Ismullah al-`Azham* that is not revealed to you, but that Beautiful Name is embedded there!

The Prophet ﷺ said:

كل عمل لم يبدأ باسم الله فهو أبتر

Any `amal which does not begin with 'Bismillahi 'r-Rahmani 'r-Raheem' is cut off; it has no continuity. *(Ahmad, al-Musnad)*

So he urged his *Sahaabah* ‎رضي الله عنهم to keep reading, "*Bismillahi 'r-Rahmani 'r-Raheem*" because it contains the Greatest Name of Allah, and the one reading it is dressed with that Holy Name without him even knowing and, therefore, it is impossible to be punished on Judgment Day when you are dressed with that Name! So for every *`amal* recite, "*A`oodhu billahi min ash-Shaytaani 'r-rajeem. Bismillahi 'r-Rahmani 'r-Raheem.* I am seeking refuge in You, *yaa Rabbee*!"

May Allah ﷻ forgive us and may Allah ﷻ bless us.

Wa min Allahi 't-tawfiq, bi ḥurmati 'l-ḥabīb, bi ḥurmati 'l-Fātiḥah.

And with Allah is success. For the sake of the Beloved, for his sake we recite the opening chapter of Holy Qur'an.

The Key to Open All Things is Knowledge of Ismullah al-`Azham

A'ūdhu billāhi min ash-Shayṭāni 'r-rajīm. Bismillāhi' r-Raḥmāni 'r-Raḥīm.
Nawaytu 'l-arbā'īn, nawaytu 'l-'itikāf, nawaytu'l-khalwah, nawaytu 'l-'uzlah,
nawaytu 'r-riyāḍa, nawaytu 's-sulūk, lillāhi Ta'alā fī hādhā 'l-masjid.
Atī'ūllāha wa atī'ū 'r-Rasūla wa ūlī 'l-amri minkum.
Obey Allah, obey the Prophet, and obey those in authority among you. (4:59)

Dastūr, madad yā Sulṭān al-Awlīyā, Mawlana Shaykh Nazim al-Haqqani ق.
Dastūr, madad yā Sulṭān al-Awlīyā, Mawlana Shaykh 'AbdAllah ad-Daghestani ق.

Bismillahi 'r-Rahmani 'r-Raheem! If you want to open a lock, you need *Bismillahi 'r-Rahmani 'r-Raheem.* It is the key for Paradise! Everything has a key and, therefore, every Paradise must have a key. The key Allah ﷻ has given to the Prophet ﷺ for Paradises is *Bismillahi 'r-Rahmani 'r-Raheem.*

In it is the Greatest Name of Allah ﷻ; three Names are there: "Allah," "ar-Rahman" and "ar-Raheem." Allah's Greatest Name is embedded in these three names, so whoever reads *"Bismillahi 'r-Rahmani 'r-Raheem,"* the Greatest Name of Allah ﷻ will be manifest directly to them and for each person it is not the same.

The Prophet ﷺ said that his *Rawdah* and his house are a piece of Paradise:

ما بين قبري و منبري روضة من رياض الجنة

Between my grave and my pulpit is rawdatan min riyaadu'l-jannah, a garden from the Gardens of Paradise. (Bukhari and Muslim)

If people can recall, thirty to forty years ago when you entered the *Rawdah* there was a grille on the left side. Now there are mostly shelves there to put the Qur'an and they block the door of the Holy Grave of the Prophet ﷺ. If you approached the *Rawdah* from the back, on the left side where you pray towards the *qiblah*, the Holy Grave of the Prophet ﷺ is there and there is a door next to the window called, *"Baab at-Tawbah,"* the Door of Repentance. We were ordered by Grandshaykh ق to stand by that door and read the *adab* of the *Tariqah*. We used to read the *awraad* standing and pray by that door as close as we could get, until we reached the threshold.

It has an old-style Ottoman lock. Every holy month the Sultan used to come, stand by the door and say, "*Bismillahi 'r-Rahmani 'r-Raheem*," and if he was a pious Sultan, the lock would open by itself! Then the Sultan used to enter crawling on his chest and cleaning the inside of the Holy Grave with rose essence from Isparta, Turkey, where the whole city is filled with flowers. They used to bring rose essence in big buckets or containers, and the king went by himself and cleaned it. The lock opened only for a pious king or deputy who would say, "*Bismillahi 'r-Rahmani 'r-Raheem*," because it has the secret of *Ismullah al-`Azham*, which is the key for everything! If it opens locks in Paradise, will it not open them in *dunya*?

The Prophet ﷺ said, from what Allah ﷻ told him directly:

كنت كنزا مخفياً فأحببت أن أعرف فخلقت الخلق

I was a Hidden Treasure (and) I wanted to be known, so I created Creation.

(Hadith Qudsi)

That treasure is *Ismullah al-`Azham*, the Greatest Name of Allah ﷻ, which is hidden and unknown. *Baab at-Tawbah* is the balance or the proof of who is pious and who is not. Sometimes those who are not pious don't dare to go there and be humiliated if the door doesn't open, so they keep back.

*Ismullah al-`Azham* is in these three Beautiful Names and the *awliyaullah* say that the Greatest Name came in the *awaa'il as-soor*, the first verses of each *surah* of the Holy Qur'an. To give an example, when Jibreel ؑ came to the Prophet ﷺ reciting, he said, "*Kaf*," and the Prophet ﷺ said, "`*Alimtu*. I knew it!" so Jibreel didn't continue. Usually when you recite Surah Maryam, you recite, "*Kaf. Ha. Ya. `Ayn. Saad*," but he recited each letter separately, and each time he recited one letter the Prophet ﷺ said, "I knew." When the Prophet ﷺ said that he knew *Kaf*, it means whatever words begin with *Kaf* the Prophet ﷺ knows, and the meanings behind them. What is highest meaning behind the letter *Kaf*? It is, "*Kun!*" His Order "Be!" is fulfilled as soon as He wills it; He says, "*Kaf*" and it happens!

Kaf is also, *kuntu kanzan makhfiyyan*, "I was a Hidden Treasure." So when you say "*Kaf*," all the secrets of Creation will come to you! *Awliyaullah* use that; when they say "*Kaf*," they take drops of meaning from that ocean of the Prophet ﷺ. When they want to know about Creation or anyone in it, they say *"Kaf!"*

"Ha" is *ghayban mutlaq, Huwa,* The Absolute Unknown. *Qul yaa Muhammad Huwa*! He is the Absolute Unknown: known through His Beautiful Names and Attributes, but unknown through His Essence. Allah's Beautiful Names and Attributes are some Names and some Descriptions of the Essence. *Ar-Rahman* and *ar-Raheem* belong to the Essence. Some are descriptions, like, *"an-Noor"* and *"as-Saboor."* Attributes describe the Essence and Names name the Essence.

Allah ﷻ put three of His Names, not Attributes, in *"Bismillahi 'r-Rahmani 'r-Raheem,"* which contains *Ismullah al-`Azham,* so by reading it every day, things begin to happen as you want them. If we don't see anything happening, even after we say, *"Bismillahi 'r-Rahmani 'r-Raheem"* and make *du`a,* that is because it only happens if you have *hudoor al-qalb,* presence of the heart. To access that power requires more than just saying the words. Like we recite *du`a*s or the Holy Qur'an daily and yet see nothing of these knowledges because they are hidden, because we don't yet have *hudoor,* presence! *Inna lid-du`ai adaabin wa sharaait,* from making *du`a* is good manners and conditions.

Ikhlaas is a condition: without it there will be no answer in *dunya,* but it will be answered in *Akhirah* and in the grave. Allah ﷻ postpones it until you are most in need of the benefit of these *du`as* and they are kept by the Prophet ﷺ as a trust for you as otherwise, when you commit a sin Shaytan takes that away from you. So instead, the Prophet ﷺ keeps them in a trust and they are given to everyone on the Day of Judgment.

دَعَوُا اللَّهَ مُخْلِصِينَ لَهُ الدِّينَ

Da`oo Allaaha mukhliseena lahu 'd-deen.

They call to Allah, offering Him sincere devotion. *(Surat Luqman, 31:32)*

But if you are a pious person, one who is *fa da`oollaha mukhliseena lahu 'd-deen,* calling on Allah and sincere in your religion, when we make *du`a* we memorized it because it does not come to us spontaneously, and we blend them, which is okay, but *awliyaullah* don't make a *du`a* by blending them from here and there. For us to understand the reality of *du`a,* I'll tell this story.

Grandshaykh, may Allah ﷻ bless his soul, went in seclusion for one year in Madinah. Usually in *khalwah* students are not kept with the teacher, because the student will faint from the *tajalli* coming on the guide. But he said, *khariqan lil asbaab,* contrary to the norm, an order came from the Prophet ﷺ for Grandshaykh ق to bring Mawlana Shaykh Nazim ق in his room to do *khalwah* with him.

Mawlana Shaykh Nazim ق was allowed to go to *Masjid an-Nabawi* for the five daily prayers and return on one condition: that his eyes would always remain on his feet. He focused his gaze on where he walked as he was not allowed to look far. Mawlana Shaykh ق said that Grandshaykh ق did not sleep for one year! As we said before, when you enter these Oceans of Knowledge, if you ever feel sleepy, for forty days maintain the practice of making *wudu* and praying two *raka`ats,* and after that you will not need sleep, your body will accommodate itself. That is for *awliyaullah.*

Mawlana Shaykh Nazim ق said Grandshaykh ق made *du`a* for one, two or three hours and never from memory; his *du`a* came spontaneously like a fountain from his heart. His heart give to the mind and the mind to the tongue. He said Grandshaykh's *du`a* made the whole area shake, as if the whole world trembled from his *du`a*! Then at the end of seclusion they heard some voices crying, the way children cry behind their father and mother. That is *fa da`oollaha mukhliseena lahu 'd-deen,* calling on Allah ﷻ with sincerity in religion that the Prophet ﷺ brought.

At the end of the seclusion when they could speak, Mawlana Shaykh ق asked, "O my Master, what are these voices?" And Grandshaykh ق said, "These voices are Iblees *wa junoodahu,* they are crying because *falatna min,* not in their hands anymore." Grandshaykh ق and Mawlana Shaykh Nazim ق are no longer in hands of Iblees, by the sincerity they showed in one year. Iblees and his groups were crying, "O they ran away from us and we cannot catch them anymore, they are gone!"

All of this was because of sincerity. The *du`as* that Grandshaykh ق used to make were not from memory, but were spontaneous. That *ikhlaas* took away veils. It was as if he was reading the teleprompter and seeing these letters and words of light. He read *du`as* that were never heard before!

So when the Prophet ﷺ said "*Kaf,*" he did not need to continue any further, if he continued, it would be *maa laa ya`nee,* needless. He understood, and there was no need to explain any more, as precious time would be wasted. (In *tasawwuf* or spirituality, you cannot say or do anything that wastes time.) He told Jibreel ؑ not to continue since he knew it already. How? When Jibreel ؑ said "*Kaf*" and "*Ha,*" the Prophet ﷺ knew. These are keywords. The *Ismullah al-`Azham* is between the abbreviations, which are these letters. Some *surahs* have the letters *"Ha"* and *"Meem"* or other abbreviated letters at their beginning.

If you are *mukhlis* your *du`a* will be answered, otherwise not. There are some *awliyaullah* who are sincere and their *du`a* is answered, but not all the time. Some people come with difficult illnesses that are removed with *du`a,* but sometimes not. Some people who don't have children come and you make *du`a* for them and the wife gets pregnant, but you make *du`a* for others and nothing happens. If you are sincere, then why sometimes the *du`a* works and sometimes it doesn't? This is to tell the *wali* who is praying that this is in Allah's Hands and to be humble!

One of the *qutbs,* `Ubaydullah al-Ahrar ق, was passing from this life and said, "When I leave *dunya,* take my turban and throw it in the air. Whosever head it lands on will be my *khAlifah."* All his *mureeds* were big scholars, so they all wanted to be *khAlifah.* When they threw the turban, it went to the shoe valet at the back of the *masjid* who was putting everyone's shoes in line and polishing them, because when people come to the *masjid* they throw the shoes on the side, which is not *adab.* Some people come at the back and arrange them nicely; they are better than you! If they don't arrange the shoes, who will do it? Not the peacocks!

رب اشعث اغبر لو اقسم على الله لأبره

There may be a disheveled, dusty person who, if he swears an oath by Allah, Allah will fulfill it. *(Muslim)*

That is a real sincere one, not the one who shouts to show he is in complete *dhikr,* but rather he is screaming at the top of his voice, *"Naray takbeer*!" without his heart being present. So the important thing is, if you want to yell and scream make your heart present in the love of Allah ﷻ and the Prophet ﷺ. At the moment when the heart is present with the Intercessor, if you have *ikhlaas* that presence becomes the intercessor for you and if you don't have *ikhlaas* it is a waste of time.

And he says, "It has been revealed that there is a Greatest Name of Allah ﷻ, an *Ismullah al-`Azham."* This has become famous between the *ummah* and everyone is pleased to know about its benefits, but it has been covered and forbidden to be discussed anywhere because you cannot give diamonds to children, you give them candy! If you know the *Ismullah al-`Azham,* you can say, *kun fayakoon,* "'Be' and it is!"

The Qur'an mentions Sayyidina Musa ﷺ saying:

قَالَ رَبِّ أَرِنِي أَنظُرْ إِلَيْكَ قَالَ لَن تَرَانِي وَلَـٰكِنِ انظُرْ إِلَى الْجَبَلِ فَإِنِ اسْتَقَرَّ مَكَانَهُ فَسَوْفَ تَرَانِي فَلَمَّا تَجَلَّى رَبُّهُ لِلْجَبَلِ جَعَلَهُ دَكًّا وَخَرَّ موسَى صَعِقًا فَلَمَّا أَفَاقَ قَالَ سُبْحَانَكَ تُبْتُ إِلَيْكَ وَأَنَا أَوَّلُ الْمُؤْمِنِينَ

Qaala rabbee arinee anzhur ilayk, qaala lan taraanee wa laakin unzhur ila 'l-jabali, fa in istaqarrra makaanuhu fa-sawfa taraanee, fa lamaa tajalla rabbuhu li 'l-jabali ja`alahoo dakkan wa kharra Moosa sa`iqan, falamma afaaqa qaala subhaanaka tubtu ilayk, wa anaa awwal al-mu'mineen.

He said, "O my Lord! Show Yourself to me, that I may look upon You." Allah said, "By no means can you see Me (directly), but look upon the mountain; if it abides in its place, then you shall see Me." When his Lord manifested His glory on the mount, He made it as dust, and Moses fell down in a swoon. When he recovered his senses, he said, "Glory be to You! To You I return in repentance, and I am the first to believe." *(Surat al-`Araaf, 7:143)*

He said, *"Arinee anzhur ilayk."* He wanted to know the *Ismullah al-`Azham* in order to say *"Kun fayakoon!"* He knew that he couldn't see Allah ﷻ in *dunya*. So he said, *"Arinee unzhur ilayk."*

According some *tafseers*, to see something is also to know about it. For example, if you say, "I saw the moon," it also means, "I knew about the moon." Sayyidina Musa ﷺ knew he cannot see Allah ﷻ, but he was asking permission to know about Him. Allah ﷻ said he cannot see Him, so He said, "Look at the mountain. You have too much ego. Destroy that first!"

Ismullah al-`Azham* is *"khaarijin min `alam as-soowar," and we are images and pictures, and the Greatest Name is outside that world of images. You have to disappear and annihilate yourself in order to know the *Ismullah al-`Azham.* That Name is for all realities that came out from, "I was a hidden treasure and I wanted to be known." It means, "I made them to know Who is the *Ismullah al-`Azham!"* It is a unique issue from the realities that are in the World of Realities and the meanings of these realities that came from outside the world of pictures, images and forms to the World of Knowledge of Realities. The meaning of it is *al-Insaan al-Kaamil*, the Perfect Human Being!

When He said, al-*`Aqal al-Awwal*, "the First Mind," it means the highest in Creation. Who is the highest and the first one in Creation? The Prophet ﷺ is! He is *al-Insaan al-Kaamil* and the *khAlifah* who represents Allah ﷻ in Creation.

When Grandshaykh ق said that in front of my uncle, who was the head of Middle East scholars, my uncle thought. "If he will answer my seven questions, I will surrender to him." After hearing the explanation, my uncle kissed Grandshaykh's ق hands, although when he entered he only shook his hand, but when he left, he kissed them, indicating that he knew Grandshaykh ق was different from the others. *Huwa fee kulli `asr man yakhudh al-khilafah min an-nabiyy huwa mumathilan lin-Nabi* ﷺ.

In every century there is one who can carry the secret of *Ismullah al-`Azham* from the Perfect Human Being, Sayyidina Muhammad ﷺ, whom Allah ﷻ dressed with *Ismullah al-`Azham*. That is how the Prophet ﷺ reached *Qaaba Qawsayni aw Adnaa*. He keeps getting nearer and nearer, it never stops! But as near as he gets, there can never be great closeness of the Creator to the Creation. Even though that distance is so small, as the Prophet ﷺ is dressed with the *Ismullah al-`Azham,* still he is a creature and there is great difference between the Creator and the created.

Allah ﷻ dressed the Prophet ﷺ with *Ismullah al-`Azham* and it is with the power of that Name that he was able to reach *Qaaba Qawsayni aw Adnaa.* He went forward when Jibreel ﵇ could not. Even the *Buraaq* was not carrying him forward. He moved forward by himself and that was by the power of *Ismullah al-`Azham.* We will open from that tomorrow: how the Prophet ﷺ recited *"Bismillahi 'r-Rahmani 'r-Raheem."*

May Allah ﷻ forgive us and may Allah ﷻ bless us.

Wa min Allahi 't-tawfiq, bi ḥurmati 'l-ḥabīb, bi ḥurmati 'l-Fātiḥah.

And with Allah is success. For the sake of the Beloved, for his sake we recite the opening chapter of Holy Qur'an.

The Secret of Allah's Greatest Name

A'ūdhu billāhi min ash-Shayṭāni 'r-rajīm. Bismillāhi' r-Raḥmāni 'r-Raḥīm.
Nawaytu 'l-arbā'īn, nawaytu 'l-'itikāf, nawaytu'l-khalwah, nawaytu 'l-'uzlah,
nawaytu 'r-riyāḍa, nawaytu 's-sulūk, lillāhi Ta'alā fī hādhā 'l-masjid.
Atī'ūllāha wa atī'ū 'r-Rasūla wa ūlī 'l-amri minkum.
Obey Allah, obey the Prophet, and obey those in authority among you. (4:59)

Dastūr, madad yā Sulṭān al-Awlīyā, Mawlana Shaykh Nazim al-Haqqani ق.
Dastūr, madad yā Sulṭān al-Awlīyā, Mawlana Shaykh 'AbdAllah ad-Daghestani ق.

Allah! *As-salaamu `alaykum wa rahmatullah wa barakatuh! Mashaa-Allah. 'Qalqala'* means "the right word," but scholars now only know *'laqlaqa,'* which has no meaning. *Bismillahi 'r-Rahmani 'r-Raheem. Allahumma salli wa sallim `alaa Sayyidina Muhammad wa `alaa aali Sayyidina Muhammad.*

When we make *du`a*, we say *tahmeed, "Alhamdulillah rabbi 'l `alameen as-salaatu wa 's-salaamu `alayka ayyuha 'n-nabi...,"* then we continue the *du`a*, but the Prophet ﷺ said, *"Du`a is never rejected when it begins with "Bismillahi 'r-Rahmani 'r-Raheem."* Why? Because it contains three of Allah's Precious Beautiful Names, which they say are the "Beautiful Names," to demonstrate there is no beauty in this universe or Heavens without Allah's Beautiful Names and Attributes. Allah's Names make everything beautiful! When Allah ﷻ created the Pen, He ordered it to write *Laa ilaaha illa-Llah Muhammadun Rasoolullah,* "There is no creator except Allah and Muhammad is His Messenger." So whatever the Prophet ﷺ says is real, *laa shak wa laa shubha,* without objection or doubt.

Who among the *Sahaabah* ؓ never had doubt about what the Prophet ﷺ said? Anything the Prophet ﷺ said, Sayyidina Abu Bakr as-Siddiq ؓ said, *"Sadaqta, yaa Rasoolullah."* You know the message came to a people who were unaware of Islam, so when it came, some principles were too much for them, like the story of the *Mi`raaj*. On his return, the Prophet ﷺ stood on a hill and said, "Last night I went for *Israa' wa 'l-Mi`raaj." 'Israa"* means that he moved at night across *hadd ad-dunya, saraa fi 'l-layl.*

Hearing this news, the *Sahaabah* ؓ vacillated between acceptance and denial, but Sayyidina Abu Bakr as-Siddiq ؓ immediately said, *"Sadaqta yaa Rasoolullah*! Yes, what you said is the truth," because Sayyidina Muhammad

ﷺ and Sayyidina Abu Bakr as-Siddiq ؓ shared a mutual love. So when the Prophet ﷺ approached *Qaaba Qawsayni aw Adnaa* he was not afraid, but he felt the loneliness of the situation and wanted familiarity to feel okay. So Allah made him hear the movement and feel the presence of Sayyidina Abu Bakr as-Siddiq ؓ; then he became *atma'ana Rasoolullah, mutma'in,* tranquil, because he sensed a friend was with him.

That is why when someone dies he is worried and feels *khashiya,* fear of Allah, fear of what is going to happen, as he is alone and has no family with him. That is why some people say to leave the light on in the room he is in, as his soul comes back to the house where he died to get *uns,* familiarity. That is why the Prophet ﷺ said, "I will be shoulder-to-shoulder in the grave with the *mu'min* who remembered me in *dunya* to give him a feeling of familiarity." That is because when Prophet ﷺ was in *Qaaba Qawsayni aw Adnaa,* Allah ﷻ made him hear the sound of Sayyidina Abu Bakr as-Siddiq ؓ and then he relaxed, which is how he knew Prophet ﷺ was in the *Mi`raaj,* so upon hearing the announcement he quickly said, *"Sadaqta yaa Rasoolullah!"*

Sayyidina `Umar ؓ received knowledge and advice from both Sayyidina Abu Bakr as-Siddiq ؓ and Sayyidina `Ali ؓ and it is well known that were it not for Sayyidina `Ali ؓ, Sayyidina `Umar ؓ would have made two mistakes in his decisions. So whatever you do in your life you must say, *"Bismillahi 'r-Rahmani 'r-Raheem"* as *Ismullah al-`Azham* is in it. If anyone truly knows what *Ismullah al-`Azham* is, he can say, *"Kun! Fayakoon"* and that will come into existence!

When Allah created Creation, He dressed them with the Reality of *Ismullah al-`Azham.* Whom did He dress? Prophet ﷺ was the first to be created, so Allah dressed the Light of the Prophet ﷺ with the Reality of *Ismullah al-`Azham.* So when you look at the Prophet ﷺ you see the Light of *Ismullah al-`Azham,* and for that reason he didn't shatter when the Qur'an was revealed to him, because *Ismullah al-`Azham* is in the Qur'an so he was able to carry it.

Grandshaykh ق said, and I quote here from his notes:

> According to the hadith, Prophet ﷺ said that every *mu'min* in the highest level of Paradise will see Allah ﷻ. What Prophet ﷺ meant by this was also in accordance with what we know, that nothing can contain Allah. So how can we see Him? Allah ﷻ dresses the Prophet ﷺ, *al-Insaan al-Kaamil,* with three-thousand of Allah's Beautiful Names and Attributes, and afterwards manifests His Greatest Name on him, *Ismullah al-`Azham,* dressing the Prophet ﷺ with that Light. People see it

and feel they saw Allah ﷻ, although that is impossible because Allah cannot be seen; even the Prophet ﷺ, who reached *Qaaba Qawsayni aw Adnaa*--two bows' length or less near the Divine Presence--still cannot see The Essence. He can see Allah's Beautiful Names and Attributes, but He cannot see the Reality of The Essence. He can see what emanates from The Essence, manifestations of not only those three-thousand Beautiful Names, but all of them!

We already explained the three-thousand Beautiful Names and Attributes, that ﷻ Allah made known: one-thousand to His Angels, one-thousand to His Prophets, three-hundred are in the *Zaboor*, three-hundred in the *Injeel* and three-hundred in the *Tawraat,* ninety-nine in the Holy Qur'an, and all these Names are in the Qur'an. The Ninety-nine Beautiful Names and Attributes are the heart of these three-thousand Names, and *Ismullah al-`Azham* is the heart of the Ninety-nine Beautiful Names and Attributes.

So the Light of *Ismullah al-`Azham* will manifest on the Prophet ﷺ and shine on that Paradise, and through the Perfect One, Sayyidina Muhammad ﷺ, those Lights will appear and who is in that Paradise will see it on him and think it is Allah Himself. Allah lets them feel He is appearing, but actually His Light appears because no one can carry His Original Appearance, which is from *al-Noor,* from which everything comes into light. If there is no light in this room you could not see anything here, but when there is *noor* you can see everything.

Grandshaykh ق continues:

Then Allah ﷻ orders the Prophet ﷺ to send the *mu'mins* who are in this Paradise to go one after another to different levels of Paradise carrying that *Noor*. They are dressed with the Light of *Ismullah al-`Azham* from the Light that is dressed on the Prophet ﷺ, and when they appear, the people of that Paradise think they are seeing Allah ﷻ, while in reality it is the *mu'min* who appears from the Paradise of *Muhammadiyoon,* shining with that Light the Prophet ﷺ dressed them with:

ما وسعني أرضي ولا سمائي ولكن وسعني قلب عبدي المؤمن

Neither My Heavens nor My Earth contain Me, but the heart of My Believing Servant contains Me. (*Hadith Qudsi, Al-Ihya* of Imam al-Ghazali)

There is no way that anything can contain Me, but the Noor that *waqara fee qalb Abu Bakr as-Siddiq al-ladhee fadalla...ghayri,* as described by the hadith, that Light is in the heart of Abu Bakr as-Siddiq ؓ and that's why he is different from everyone else and favored the most, because that Light comes from that secret in his heart that he was carrying from Prophet ﷺ. Prophet ﷺ sent traces of the *Ismullah al-`Azham* to Sayyidina Abu Bakr as-Siddiq ؓ and Sayyidina `Ali ؓ.

أنا مدينة العلم و علي بابه

I am the City of Knowledge and `Ali is its Door (or Gate).

(al-Haakim, Tirmidhi)

Sayyidina `Ali ؓ was at the door, but didn't enter inside because that is reserved for Sayyidina Abu Bakr as-Siddiq ؓ; however, you cannot go inside without Sayyidina `Ali ؓ. These three Names, *"ar-Rahmaan," "ar-Raheem"* and "Allah" are the Names Allah likes best. They are from *ad-Dhaat*, the Essence, and they are not *Siffat*, Attributes, but they are not describing the Attributes. *"Ar-Rahmaan"* that is from His Mercy that He gives everyone what they want, both the *mu'min* and non-*mu'min*. *"Al-Kareem,"* the Generous One, will not take back any gift He gave, just a *mu'min* does not take back any gift he gave. So under that *Siffat ar-Rahmah*, Allah gives.

Allah ﷻ said:

الرَّحْمَنُ عَلَّمَ الْقُرْآنَ

Ar-Rahmaan `alam al-Qur'an.

The Most Merciful has imparted this Qur'an. *(Surat ar-Rahmaan, 55:1,2)*

He didn't say, *"Allah ar-Rahmaan `alam al-Qur'an."* He created many Names that describe that *"Ism ar-Rahmaan."*

Prophet ﷺ said Allah ﷻ has one-hundred Mercies:

U`tiya waahidan minhaa ila ahlu 'd-dunya.

Allah gave the Prophet ﷺ one of these ninety-nine to all human beings.

'Ahlu 'd-Dunya' does not only include human beings, but also *ins, jinn* and all created beings in this universe. From *Ism ar-Rahmaan*, Allah created one-hundred Names to describe that Name, and *dunya* is under only one of them. Allah provides for *Ahlu 'd-Dunya*, and He left ninety-nine Names of *Rahmat* other than the Ninety-Nine Beautiful Names and Attributes, about which the Prophet ﷺ said, "Allah has Ninety-Nine Names use them to call

on Him." Of the Ninety-nine Names of *rahmah,* everyone is under that *rahmah* as Allah ﷻ is providing us whatever we are getting in *dunya*: life, breath, cures, food....

Why did He keep the other ninety-nine Names of *rahmah,* why He didn't send them to *dunya*? Because everyone would faint from all of them. This whole *dunya* got all that is here from one of them and we cannot carry more than that. Why did Allah order us to make *salawaat* on the Prophet ﷺ? Why did Allah say, "I am making *salawaat* and all My Angels are making *salawaat,* so you believers also make *salawaat.*" Allah ﷻ did that to create a cause for Him to give His Mercy, so He is sending *rahmah* with His *Salawaat* to raise the Prophet ﷺ higher and higher!

When we make *salawaat,* Allah ﷻ increases us with what He increases the Prophet ﷺ, which we explained in the recent series *Salawat of Tremendous Blessings* (2012), at the beginning of Ramadan. For example, *Salawaat al-Faatih* is one line only, and when Muhammad al-Talmaysani ؓ completed reading *Dalaa'il al-Khayraat* 100,000 times, the Prophet ﷺ appeared to him in a dream saying, "O Muhammad al-Talmaysani! If you recite *Salawaat al-Faatih,* it will be as if you recited *Dalaa'il al-Khayraat* 800,000 times!" So if you recite this *salawaat* three times before you sleep, it will be as if you recited *Dalaa'il al-Khayraat* 2,400,000 times!

Allah ﷻ reserved the ninety-nine Names of Mercy because if He gave them all now the whole *dunya* would faint, so He kept them for *Akhirah.* He will dress Sayyidina Muhammad ﷺ with the ninety-nine Names of *Rahmah.* So that is why there must be traces of *Ismullah al-`Azham* in these three Names, "Allah," "*ar-Rahmaan*" and "*ar-Raheem,*" which is why the Prophet ﷺ ordered us to recite "*Bismillahi 'r-Rahmani 'r-Raheem*" with *Surat al-Fatihah.* That is equal to reciting the entire Holy Qur'an, as is reading "*Qul huwa Allahu Ahad*" three times.

Previously, Allah did not allow any understanding of *Ismullah al-`Azham,* as there was no one able to understand that, but in the no-time zone when Allah created the Prophet ﷺ, in *`Alam ar-Rawhaniyaat,* the World of Meanings, Allah introduced him to *Bismillahi 'r-Rahmani 'r-Raheem.* And when the World of Images... didn't reveal to Sayyidina Musa ؑ or any other Prophet, but when the Prophet ﷺ came to this *dunya* from the World of Images to... then Allah dressed him with the Light of His Beautiful Names and Attributes, *Ismullah al-`Azham,* which only the Prophet ﷺ knows and *awliyaullah* can detect, but in a minimal way.

This knowledge is not in books, but rather it is in Grandshaykh's and Mawlana Shaykh Nazim's hearts, and they give information. Grandshaykh ق was like a fountain whenever he opened these subjects and it is impossible to quote everything he said.

So *'ar-Rahmaan'* is *at-tafadul wal-Ihsaan,* the Favors of Allah, Who gives from His Generosity; it means *al-`atif bi rizq al-khalq* will appoint for His Creation what they need and remove afflictions from them. *'Ar-Raheem'* is if you ask Allah accepts and if you don't He gets upset. Allah likes to give to His Servant, so when you ask, He gives!

ادْعُونِي أَسْتَجِبْ لَكُمْ

Supplicate to Me and I will give you! *(Surat al-Mu'min, 40:60)*

If you don't ask He gets angry because He takes that *siffat* out of you, that is His Anger:

وَمَا نُرْسِلُ بِالآيَاتِ إِلاَّ تَخْوِيفًا

We only send the Signs by way of terror (and warning from evil).

(Surat al-Israa', 17:59)

"We don't send the Verses of Punishment except to make people fear!" So when you read *ayats* of punishment, Allah takes that punishment away from you, if you possess those characteristics that would cause you to be punished like that. And when you recite Holy Qur'an, those verses will take this all away and Allah will dress you from His Holy Paradise. Therefore, Allah likes His Servants to ask from Him! If you don't get what you ask for in this life, you will get it in the Next Life.

If you ask He will give, and if you don't ask He gets angry. To the contrary, if you ask human beings they get angry! But Allah likes to give, so ask Him, "*Yaa Rabbee*! We are asking through Your Generosity to grant that we be with the Prophet ﷺ in *dunya,* in death, in the grave, on Resurrection, during the Account." If you don't ask from Allah ﷻ, He gets upset, so it is better to ask Him.

Who knew about these three Beautiful Names and Attributes, "Allah," "*ar-Rahmaan*" and "*ar-Raheem,*" and what description they contain, of which we are describing here only in a very limited understanding, not is a professional way, as *awliyaullah* are not professional. So if you recite "*Bismillahi 'r-Rahmani 'r-Raheem,*" it is as if you mentioned Allah ﷻ with all

His Beautiful Names and Attributes! Also, whoever recites them will be dressed with all these three-thousand Beautiful Names and Attributes as if he made *dhikr* with them and knew all the infinite number of Allah's Beautiful Names and Attributes! That will be dressed on you if you recite *"Bismillahi 'r-Rahmani 'r-Raheem"* even once.

And it is related in reports and in the *Seerah* that Prophet ﷺ said, "On the night of *Israa' wa 'l-Mi`raaj*, Allah made me see all Paradises." He did not say "seven Paradises;" he did not limit them, which means there are more than seven. Also, Paradises cannot carry who will describe that and who will enter it. There are special Paradises and *inshaa-Allah* Allah will put us there. So when Prophet ﷺ saw these Paradises, he saw four flowing rivers: one was a river of crystal water condensed from the water's coolness, and then a river of wine and a river of honey.

According to Grandshaykh's notes, Prophet ﷺ said, "*Yaa* Jibreel! From where do these rivers come and to where are they going?"

Sayyidina Jibreel عليه السلام replied, "All these rivers come from the highest Paradise and then the ninety-nine Paradises unite and blend in that ocean."

What is that ocean Jibreel عليه السلام is mentioning? The Prophet ﷺ was waiting for the answer, which is only for us to learn as Prophet ﷺ already knew. That ocean is *Multaqa al-Bahrayn*, the confluence of those four rivers, known as *Hawd al-Kawthar*, about which Allah ﷻ said: *inna `ataynaaka 'l-kawthar*. Where they meet is a beautiful blending of water, milk, honey, and wine, which we have never tasted! *Inshaa-Allah* we will taste it in Paradise!

Prophet ﷺ said, "*Yaa* Jibreel! From where does it come?"

Sayyidina Jibreel عليه السلام said, "I don't know from where it comes, except that it comes from these four places. O Muhammad! Ask Allah to teach you from where these rivers come."

So the Prophet ﷺ immediately asked, or otherwise Allah would have been upset. As soon as he asked, an angel responsible for all those rivers came, greeted Prophet ﷺ and said, "Close your eyes, *yaa* Muhammad," and then, "Open your eyes."

Prophet explained, "I opened my eyes and saw a tree and a dome made of pearl, *Qubbat al-Arzaaq*, the Dome of Provisions.

The root of the Arabic word for water, *"maa`a,"* is the letter *meem*. When Jibreel عليه السلام offered the Prophet ﷺ milk, wine and water, he chose milk. So the wine is coming from the *meem* of *al-Rahmaan* and honey is coming from the *meem* of *ar-Rahmaan*, and from this knowledge Prophet ﷺ said,

"Then I knew these four rivers come from someone who says *'Bismillahi 'r-Rahmani 'r-Raheem.'"* So say *"Bismillahi 'r-Rahmani 'r-Raheem!" Inshaa-Allah,* may Allah ﷻ make us drink from these four rivers!

Also, Allah ﷻ said, "O Muhammad! Whoever, without any desire of being seen, mentioned Me by saying *'Bismillahi 'r-Rahmani 'r-Raheem,'* I will make him drink from these four rivers and his *du`a* will never be rejected if it begins with *'Bismillahi 'r-Rahmani 'r-Raheem.'*

O Allah! For the sake of *Bismillahi 'r-Rahmani 'r-Raheem,* forgive us and accept from us Ramadan on the last day, and take away from us all difficulties in health or wealth.

May Allah ﷻ forgive us and may Allah ﷻ bless us.

Wa min Allahi 't-tawfiq, bi ḥurmati 'l-ḥabīb, bi ḥurmati 'l-Fātiḥah.

And with Allah is success. For the sake of the Beloved, for his sake we recite the opening chapter of Holy Qur'an.

Seek Forgiveness and You Shall Be Forgiven

A'ūdhu billāhi min ash-Shayṭāni 'r-rajīm. Bismillāhi' r-Raḥmāni 'r-Raḥīm.
Nawaytu 'l-arbā'īn, nawaytu 'l-'itikāf, nawaytu'l-khalwah, nawaytu 'l-'uzlah,
nawaytu 'r-riyāḍa, nawaytu 's-sulūk, lillāhi Ta'alā fi hādhā 'l-masjid.
Atī'ūllāha wa atī'ū 'r-Rasūla wa ūlī 'l-amri minkum.
Obey Allah, obey the Prophet, and obey those in authority among you. (4:59)

Dastūr, madad yā Sulṭān al-Awlīyā, Mawlana Shaykh Nazim al-Haqqani ق.
Dastūr, madad yā Sulṭān al-Awlīyā, Mawlana Shaykh 'AbdAllah ad-Daghestani ق.

This is the last day of Ramadan and we are asking for Allah's forgiveness. From two words, imagine how great Allah's Mercy is and imagine how much it encompasses everything! Just remember two words that are very light on the tongue and very heavy on the Scale, even heavier than all your sins, so with them all your sins are erased: *SubhaanAllah wa bihamdihi subhaanAllahi l-`Azheem astaghfirullah.*

كلمتان خفيفتان على اللسان ثقيلتان فى الميزان حبيبتان إلى الرحمن سبحان الله و بحمده سبحان الله العظيم

The Prophet ﷺ said, "There are two words that are very easy to say, yet very heavy on the Scale, most beloved to The Merciful: SubhaanAllah wa bihamdihi subhaanAllahi 'l-`Azheem."

This phrase is heavier than any sin ever committed in your life, and everything will be waived on the scale, by saying this phrase one time. However, take it as a tool, because people have become professional in continuing to make sins! *Asbah ... fee kathrat adh-dhunoob.* When one commits a sin, it becomes like his profession. He might stop for one day and then begin again the next day. What you have to do to become more professional in avoiding sins is to recite words to save you, which will be your way to safety.

For example, you might go on a highway where gangsters might be ready to attack, and certainly you would take precaution to avoid running into them. In your daily life, it is as if a lot of gangsters are facing you: *Shaytaan* and his army! What precautions should you take against these gangsters? The police take guns to protect people from them. Allah ﷻ tells us to recite the phrase, *"SubhaanAllah wa bihamdihi subhaanAllahi 'l-`Azheem istaghfirullah,"* as it will save you from *Shaytaan wa junoodahu,* Shaytan and his army.

You have to remember, the angels on your shoulders are observing what you are doing, one on the right and one on left. The angel on the right immediately records when you do something good. The one on the left does not immediately write down if you do something wrong; before he writes anything down, the angel on the right will tell him to wait in case you might repent. The angel on the left will not record the sin if the person repents within in 24 hours, then the angel on the right will record his repentance as *hasanah* and add on top of it.

The Prophet ﷺ said there are four words from Holy Qur'an that whoever says them will enter Paradise. Do you want to enter Paradise? Then say these words: *"SubhaanAllah, w'alhamdulillah, wa laa ilaaha illa-Llah, w'Allahu Akbar,"* and you may add to it as some scholars say, *"wa laa hawla wa laa quwatta illa billahi 'l-`Aliyyi'l-`Azheem."* This is a guarantee of Paradise if you recite it every day!

Imagine there is a building with safety and health inspection. Allah gave you a body that is a world by itself. It doesn't function off of electricity and not on any power, but it has its own power to move your head and limbs. Who is making the head move? What makes you see? The structure of the eye is so complex that they would have to create many machines to replicate images the eye reflects! Allah ﷻ grants all this for free. Hearing with your eardrum can detect more than a seismograph that detects the slightest tremor of earthquakes deep inside the earth! The sound goes on the eardrum and beats like az-Zahra Ensemble musical drumbeats. Electromagnetic waves produce the sound you can decipher. For a PA system, an amplifier has many buttons you can fine-tune the sound to make it very sharp, and Allah gave you ears with no buttons (sound is already pretuned).

And some say all that (magnificent features of Creation) comes by itself. From where, the rooftop? It comes from one cell, *nafsin wahidatin;* Allah ﷻ created us from one cell and molded that cell in Heavens and gave it that form. He ordered Sayyidina Jibreel ﷺ to go to earth and back to Paradise one *qabda,* handful of soil. He took a handful of soil to Heavens.

Anything in Paradise will not see punishment! We are not cursed like *Iblees* was cursed; we entered Paradise and we are *muwahidoon*, and that was carried by the pure touch of Jibreel ؑ and put in Paradise. There Allah molded it and sent to it the Light of the Prophet ﷺ and from it created a human being, which is pure! Let's look at the hadith of the Prophet ﷺ:

يولد الإنسان على الفطرة

No child is born except in innocence.

(Narrated by Abu Hurayra; Bukhari, 2:23:441)

The Prophet ﷺ didn't mention Islam in this hadith; he said either his parents make him a Jew or a Christian or Zoroastrian, he didn't say that parents can make him Muslim because everyone is Muslim from beginning of Creation! Allah ﷻ didn't curse Sayyidina Adam ؑ because he repented. *Iblees* did not repent because he was jealous, so Allah didn't forgive him. Jealousy prevents you from repenting. The Light of the Prophet ﷺ was shining in the forehead of Sayyidina Adam ؑ and when he saw that, *Iblees* knew then the *Maqaam al-Mahmoud*, which he coveted for himself, would go to someone else! He thought that it would go to him because he made *sajda* in every hand span of Paradise, but Allah made his deed *habaa'an manthooraa*, like floating dust scattered about[3] and threw them in his face!

For us, Allah ﷻ said, "O My Servant! You went so far, but come back." Allah will forgive all sins. He will forgive you until your soul comes out from the last part of your life. According to scholars, *tawbah* is not accepted in those last moments, but according to *awliyaullah*, the Prophet ﷺ will be standing there beside the one who is dying and for every person who believed in *tawheed*, he ﷺ will make sure they go to Paradise!

Allah's Mercy is all-encompassing, but we must repent in order to be in it. We are in the last day of Ramadan, so we repent. Anyone who has oppressed himself by disobeying Allah ﷻ:

وَمَن يَعْمَلْ سُوءًا أَوْ يَظْلِمْ نَفْسَهُ ثُمَّ يَسْتَغْفِرِ اللَّهَ يَجِدِ اللَّهَ غَفُورًا رَّحِيمًا

---

[3] Holy Qur'an, 25:23.

Wa man y`amalu soowan aw yazhlim nafsahu thumma yastaghfirillah yajidillah ghafooran raheema.

If any one does evil or wrongs his own soul but afterwards seeks Allah's forgiveness, he will find Allah Oft-forgiving, Most Merciful.

(Surat an-Nisaa, 4:110)

This means your sins are gone by *istighfaar*! To visit the president, you have to clear security screenings and they have to check if you have an invitation or appointment, as if the president didn't come from the womb of a mother and didn't wear pampers! It takes a lot of work to see even the president's barber or the one who gives him his clothes in morning, his valet. Today stylists dress presidents and kings, and whatever they wear today is never worn again, thrown away, gone. But Allah ﷻ is saying to all of us, "Come to Me! You don't need an appointment!"

وَلَوْ أَنَّهُمْ إِذ ظَّلَمُوا أَنفُسَهُمْ جَآؤُوكَ فَاسْتَغْفَرُوا اللَّهَ وَاسْتَغْفَرَ لَهُمُ الرَّسُولُ لَوَجَدُوا اللَّهَ تَوَّابًا رَّحِيمًا

Wa law annahum idh zhaalamoo anfusahum ja'ooka f 'astaghfaroollaaha w 'astaghfara lahumu 'r-rasoolu la-wajadoo 'Llaaha tawwaaba 'r-raheema.

If they had only, when they were unjust to themselves, come to you and asked Allah's Forgiveness, and the Messenger had asked forgiveness for them, they would have found Allah indeed Oft-returning, Most Merciful.

(Surat an-Nisa, 4:64)

On that spiritual highway you can go full speed like a rocket, just by saying, "*Astaghfirullah.*" If you have remorse or regret, it is because you have *nadam,* because you feel bad about what you've done in your life. You become 70 years old and Allah still is generous with you, giving you health and wealth. You might think to yourself that you regret all the wrong things you did throughout your life, and you might ask, "How am I going to face my Lord?" That feeling of remorse is enough to be granted Allah's Forgiveness! You are coming to Him with regret. If that inspiration comes to your heart, how much does it affect your life? It means you have done something wrong, and we all have done many things wrong. We pretend that we are angels coming from Paradise when actually we are molded with arrogance, pride, jealousy, hatred, possessiveness and all kinds of bad characters. We've counted seventeen bad characteristics found in human beings. No one can say that he did not commit a sin during his life. We must remember, the door is open to repent. Allah ﷻ, with His Mercy, has forgiven a lot of *mudhnibeen* and even turned them in to *awliyaullah*! They might have done one thing in their life which Allah liked, so he turned them into a *wali.*

It is said that al-Fudayl was a highway robber who attacked people on the road and stole from travelers, and whenever he found nothing he beat them violently. But Allah ﷻ forgave him for something small he did. One day he was robbing and saw a beautiful slave girl, a *jariya,* and his heart was attracted to her.

An Arabic proverb states:

Nazhra f'abtisaman fa mawidan faliqaan fa tazawajan.

First a look, then a smile, then a date, then a meeting, then a marriage!

Without marriage that relationship is *haraam,* so do you want *halaal* or *haraam*? *Alhamdulillah,* all of you are married. To see his girlfriend, what did he so? He climbed the walls to reach her room. Once when he was climbing the tree or a wall to reach her room, he heard a voice saying:

أَلَمْ يَأْنِ لِلَّذِينَ آمَنُوا أَن تَخْشَعَ قُلُوبُهُمْ لِذِكْرِ اللَّهِ

Is it not time that the hearts of all who have attained to faith should feel humble at the remem-brance of God. *(Surat al-Hadid, 57:16)*

So he felt that address to him and from that beautiful voice and recitation he fell down (unconscious). Then he took a shower and said, *yaa Rabbee, tubtu ilayk*! "O my Lord! I repent from all I did." Then he returned to his shack, not even a house, where he stayed listening, and he heard some people approaching and saying, "We must not go on this road or Fudayl might come and kill us all! We must go another way." When he heard that, he repented to Allah ﷻ a second time and went out to guide those four people on their way. Then he travelled to *Haraam an-Nabawi* and remained there until he died. That is someone who asked Allah ﷻ to forgive him when he heard Allah say, "Is it not enough?"

Grandshaykh ق used to tell the story of Ibraheem ibn Adham, who was a king in his time. He is buried near Damascus. He was womanizing, drinking, killing this one and that one, not caring about repentance nor accepting to pray and fast, but rather doing everything he thought was good to satisfy his desires. His room in the palace was covered by a very high dome and he often slept there to see the stars. Once after a night of drinking and womanizing he slept there, and when he was half asleep, he heard knocking on the dome. He realized someone was walking on it and thought, "Is this real? Who can reach there?" He was a king whose -bodyguards were stationed all over the palace, but he was drunk, so he looked up and saw someone passing.

Someone called to him, "*Yaa* Ibraheem!" by his name, not addressing him as 'King,' as if he knew him well, and that put fear in his heart. "*Yaa* Adham! Did you see a camel here?"

Ibraheem ibn Adham said, "Are you crazy? Although I am drunk, I know there is no camel on the top of my dome!"

That one (an angel) said, "I am looking for my camel that was entrusted to you on the Day of Promises when you accepted Allah as your Lord and promised to be His Servant, so give it back to me now! I am convinced I will find it, but you will never find Allah ﷻ in your condition!"

That came to Ibraheem ibn Adham's heart like a bullet. He left his kingdom, took a shower and became *azhad az-zaahideen*, the Most Ascetic of Ascetics. He did that by repenting. He looked at that dome and saw that man looking for his camel, and that one said, "I can find my camel but you cannot find your way to Allah ﷻ, so repent!"

This is the last day of Ramadan, *yarmud adh-dhunoob*, which takes away all sins. Those who didn't fast for specific reason (that we don't need to know) for every day can give one meal for a poor person; they put that money aside and give it to someone who knows poor people to give them.

To add to Grandshaykh's story, he said Allah does not like one thing from His servant. anything you do, Allah will forgive because there is nothing in it of the rights of other servants. Everything you do is between you and Allah ﷻ as you are trying to destroy Allah's rights, so that is between you and him. But one thing Allah won't forgive, and that is if you break someone's heart, either by screaming at them, attacking them or being very angry or showing jealousy. If you break someone's heart, there is no way to glue that back and no way for repentance, except on one condition: that you go to that person and ask his forgiveness! If he forgives you, then Allah ﷻ will forgive you for destroying the rights of that person by humiliating him or damaging his reputation. That is oppression, especially when you attack your parents, especially your mother, and that is what Allah hates most!

Once when I was 20 years old, my brother and I decided to go to Sham to visit Grandshaykh `AbdAllah ق, although we had a university exam the next day. Our mother was angry and said, "Where are you going? You have big exam tomorrow."

Stubbornly, we said, "We are going!"

Most people here are obstinate, stubborn.

She said, "Don't go," and we said, "We are going!" and took the car keys and drove to Damascus.

When we came to Jabal Qasyoun and went up to Grandshaykh's house, as we approached to knock on the door, he opened it. Sometimes they are tough with the words they use.

He said, "You ate dirtiness and came to me?" That is nicer than what he actually said! "*W'Allahi*, if you ever again make your mother upset, I will not open my door for you! Go ask her for forgiveness, because you broke her heart!" and he slammed the door.

How did he know; he didn't even have a telephone. We hadn't spoken any bad words to our mother, we simply said, "We are going," and she said, "No, don't go." So we went back and apologized, we studied and passed the exam, then she said, "Now you can go."

The Prophet ﷺ said:

الجنة تحت اقدام الامهات

Paradise is under the feet of the mothers.

Also, Allah ﷻ said:

وَقَضَى رَبُّكَ أَلاَّ تَعْبُدُوا إِلاَّ إِيَّاهُ وَبِالْوَالِدَيْنِ إِحْسَانًا

Wa qadaa rabbuka alaa ta`budoo illa iyyaahu wa bi 'l-waalidayni ahsaana.

Allah has decreed not to worship anyone except Me and with your mother and father to be nice with them. *(Surat al-Isra, 17:23)*

Don't say "*oof*" too much to their (parents') face. You have no right to say that "*oof*" and if you do, the Prophet ﷺ will not look at you on the Day of Judgment! Allah said, "Don't scold your parents, but speak to them with good manners." Say, "O my father, O my mother," with *adab*. Unfortunately, I am declaring that we Muslims have no discipline in that.

Disrespecting ones' parents is not from Islam, but many Muslims have no discipline and they shout at their parents and at their brothers; they don't speak nicely.

If you disagree with someone you need to follow a protocol to address that issue. People with high manners speak to others with diplomacy, in order not to hurt anyone but to get the message across. We don't have that, we only shout, which is why we have to be very careful because Allah will not forgive anyone who shouts in the face of his mother or father. You have to make them happy, even if they are not Muslim and they ask you to take them to church, you have to take them all the way to church! That is the extent of our good manners, even in dealing with a non-Muslim.

May Allah make us listen and understand, as today so many people have a lot of problems with their children ages 15-30.

May Allah ﷻ forgive us and may Allah ﷻ bless us.

Wa min Allahi 't-tawfiq, bi ḥurmati 'l-ḥabīb, bi ḥurmati 'l-Fātiḥah.

And with Allah is success. For the sake of the Beloved, for his sake we recite the opening chapter of Holy Qur'an.

Each Verse of Surat al-Fatihah Closes One Door of Hellfire

Aʿūdhu billāhi min ash-Shayṭāni 'r-rajīm. Bismillāhi' r-Raḥmāni 'r-Raḥīm.
Nawaytu 'l-arbāʿīn, nawaytu 'l-ʿitikāf, nawaytu'l-khalwah, nawaytu 'l-ʿuzlah,
nawaytu 'r-riyāḍa, nawaytu 's-sulūk, lillāhi Taʿalā fī hādhā 'l-masjid.
Atīʿūllāha wa atīʿū 'r-Rasūla wa ūlī 'l-amri minkum.
Obey Allah, obey the Prophet, and obey those in authority among you. (4:59)

Dastūr, madad yā Sulṭān al-Awlīyā, Mawlana Shaykh Nazim al-Haqqani ق.
Dastūr, madad yā Sulṭān al-Awlīyā, Mawlana Shaykh ʿAbdAllah ad-Daghestani ق.

A*llahumma salli `alaa Sayyidina Muhammad* ﷺ. Allah ﷻ *`azamat an-Nabi* ﷺ, Allah magnified the Prophet ﷺ with the highest level of magnification, *t`azheem*, and there are many proofs, but one of them is when Sayyidina Adam ﷺ committed the sin he made *sajda* and asked forgiveness for the sake of Sayyidina Muhammad ﷺ. Then question came, "How did you know about Muhammad?" and he said, "*Yaa Rabbee*! I saw his name written on every leaf in Paradise, on every door in Paradise, if we can say "door" or "leaf" or "trees;" this is how it is mentioned, but it means "on every heavenly element in Paradise his name is written."

Today they sell you gold coins that feature an image, and you say, "O, this is original, *asliyy*, not an imitation." It is pure gold, stamped ".999," because it has that image of King George or an eagle, a leaf, or anything. So everyone says, "O, this is the very top of the matter," and so they buy it. Allah ﷻ didn't put His Name or picture on a gold coin. Allah put His Name with Prophet's name! Today every Islamic scholar says you cannot have a picture of the Prophet ﷺ, but why? Was there no camera before, or no drawings of him ﷺ? Because they tried but they never succeeded, not even to begin to draw the Prophet ﷺ because he cannot be drawn! His reality is veiled, so no one can draw his picture, but you can describe his features, *shamaa'il*. Only Allah knows the true image of Prophet! Even when the *Sahaabah* ﷺ look at Prophet ﷺ, they see a different manifestation than when Allah looks him, as only Allah knows. How can you describe "*an-Noor*"?

أول ما خلق الله نور نبيك يا جابر

The first thing Allah created is the Light of your Prophet ﷺ, O Jaabir.

Why, is there any other light? Yes, there is *Noorillah*. So the description is *"noor,"* and to Allah that is a manifestation that He created the Prophet ﷺ from His Light, one manifestation or Name that He dressed on Prophet ﷺ. However, whatever form or image the *Sahaabah* ؓ saw is the *shamaa'il*, but they cannot describe what the Prophet ﷺ is like in *qaaba qawsayni aw adnaa*. When Jibreel ؈ comes to Prophet ﷺ, he sees him from his reality. Who can carry *wahiyy*? The Holy Qur'an descended on the Prophet ﷺ--who can carry that? Only he can carry it, because he is *noor*:

يَا أَيُّهَا النَّبِيُّ إِنَّا أَرْسَلْنَاكَ شَاهِدًا وَمُبَشِّرًا وَنَذِيرًا وَدَاعِيًا إِلَى اللَّهِ بِإِذْنِهِ وَسِرَاجًا مُّنِيرًا

O Prophet! Truly We have sent you as a witness. You are the one who calls people to Allah by His permission, and (you are) a shining lamp.

(Surat al-Ahzaab, 33:45-46)

Wa siraajan muneera, a lamp, a sun, a shining moon, and from his light came everything.

When Allah ﷻ created His *noor* He taught it, and the best to be taught is Holy Qur'an, Allah's Ancient Words. Behind every word and every letter are infinite numbers of letters. There was a scholar in Lebanon, my uncle, who was very well known and whose knowledge was like an encyclopedia, and he published an encyclopedia of the letters of the Holy Qur'an in 130 volumes. I remember the volume on the letter *"Alif"* because we printed it for him, although we were not able to print the rest because that was during the war in Lebanon and it was lost when they burned everything. It took him forty years to write that and his knowledge of the letter *"Alif"* was comprised of 27 volumes, each one consisting of 1,500 pages called, *"al-Marja."* And that was only one letter! That is from one scholar; not one *wali*, but one *`alim*! So what do you think, if my uncle wrote 27 volumes on one letter and there are infinite volumes in Heavens! The entire Holy Qur'an is in contained in *Surat al-Fatihah*.

Sayyidina `Ali ؓ said the Prophet ﷺ said:

قال رسول الله صلى الله عليه وسلم: «من قرأ فاتحة الكتاب فكأنما قرأ التوراة والإنجيل والزبور والفرقان»

Whoever read the Opening Chapter of the Book, it is as if he read the Torah and the New Testament and the Psalms and the Criterion [the Qur'an].

That is *Surat al-Fatihah,* which Allah ﷻ described, and some scholars say it is more than *"al-Qur'an"* because it is mentioned:

وَلَقَدْ آتَيْنَاكَ سَبْعًا مِّنَ الْمَثَانِي وَالْقُرْآنَ الْعَظِيمَ

And We have bestowed upon you the Seven Oft-repeated (verses) and the Grand Qur'an. *(Surat al-Hijr, 15:87)*

It is as if whoever recites it has been donated the weight of the earth in gold, and not only the wealth of the earth but of the entire universe, whatever exists other than the Creator, because Allah ﷻ created creations we cannot see. If the universe were all gold and someone donated all of that in jihad, which means any kind of struggle, for every verse of *Surat al-Fatihah* he recited it would be as if he had donated the entire universe's weight in gold in the Way of Allah. Because of this, Allah ﷻ forbids his body to be burned by the Hellfire.

That is why, if you say, *"Alhamdullahi Rabbi 'l-`Alameen,"* that is one *ayah.* In some *madhdhabs* they say to read each *ayah* separately, but Hanafi School says you should connect them, Shafi`i and Hanbali read with breaks, and some say to read the *Basmalah* with the verses of *Surat al-Fatihah* in sequence without a break and Allah ﷻ will give you *Hoor al-`Ayn,* the virgin maidens of Paradise.

It is mentioned by Abi Sa`eed al-Khudree ؓ, *marfu`an,* in his *tafseer* on *Surat al-Fatihah,* that Allah ﷻ sent punishment and revenge on people and on the earth because of too many sins, and on *jinn* as well. Do you think *jinn* don't have punishment? They do, and they are locked in special houses made of *noor* and they cannot come out because they are chained with the secret of that *noor.* It is a special light that comes from fire, which is not *an-Noor,* but the light from that fire chains them in a prison from which they cannot escape. Allah ﷻ sends His Punishment on earth and when a young boy or girl reads one verse from *Surat al-Fatihah,* Allah ﷻ will take all that punishment away from that group of people for forty years, because of one child reading one *ayah*! So don't be lazy, teach your children to read *Surat al-Fatihah*!

It was related that the Prophet ﷺ said:

من أتى منزله فقرأ الحمد لله سورة الفاتحة وقل هو الله أحد نفى الله عنه الفقر وكثر خير بيته حتى يفيض على جيرانه

Whoever comes to his house and recites "All praise be to Allah" Surat al-Fatihah and Surat al-Ikhlaas, Allah ﷻ will take poverty from him and give him many provisions in his house until it spreads to his neighbors.

That means there is no limit to what Allah ﷻ will send to you, both physically and spiritually, as He sent to Sayyida Maryam ﵍:

كُلَّمَا دَخَلَ عَلَيْهَا زَكَرِيَّا الْمِحْرَابَ وَجَدَ عِندَهَا رِزْقاً قَالَ يَا مَرْيَمُ أَنَّى لَكِ هَـذَا قَالَتْ هُوَ مِنْ عِندِ اللّهِ إنَّ اللّهَ يَرْزُقُ مَن يَشَاء بِغَيْرِ حِسَابٍ

Whenever he (Zakariyya) entered her prayer niche, he found with her provision. He said, "O Mary! From where does this come to you?" She said, "From Allah, for Allah provides sustenance to whom He pleases without measure." *(Surat Aali-`Imraan, 3:37)*

Every time Sayyidina Zakariyya ﵇ entered her niche, he found provision there. What is the best *rizq*? To be in the presence of Allah ﷻ and the presence of the Prophet ﷺ. The best provision is to be in the presence of the Prophet ﷺ, so that was coming to her and Sayyidina Zakariyya ﵇ was able to detect that presence. In the time of Mahdi ﵇, one bite will be enough to sustain you for forty days without snacks or three meals a day!

So the greatness of the Prophet ﷺ is that he is in *mahal tajalliyaat al-haqq bi Surat al-Fatihah*, the place of manifestation of *Surat al-Fatihah* that comes on him. It is mentioned as *"saba`a al-mathaanee"* because it has seven verses, and there are seven Hellfires and every verse will close a door to Hellfire: the first closes the first Hellfire door, the second closes the second, and so on, until the seventh verse closes the seventh door. Therefore, there is no way the nineteen angels of Hellfire can find a way to take you in. That is why *"Bismillahi 'r-Rahmani 'r-Raheem"* must be read on everything, because it consists of nineteen letters, each of which will shut one door that will no longer be able to open for you. So when you connect *"Bismillahi 'r-Rahmani 'r-Raheem"* to *Surat al-Fatihah,* each letter will close one door and each *ayah* of *Surat al-Fatihah* will lock it.

So recite, *"Bismillahi 'r-Rahmani 'r-Raheem. Alhamdulillahi rabbi 'l-`alameen. Ar-rahmani 'r-raheem. Maaliki yaawmi 'd-deen. Iyyaaka na`abudu wa iyyaaka nasta`een. Ihdina 's-sirat al-mustaqeem. Sirat al-ladheena an`amta* *`alayhim. Ghayri 'l-maghdoobi `alayhim wa laa 'd-daaleen. Ameen.* Now with Prophet's *barakah,* we have shut the seven doors of Hellfire and took away the power from these nineteen angels of Hellfire so they will not push us into the Fire, because of the *barakah* of *Bismillahi 'r-Rahmani 'r-Raheem* and *Surat al-Fatihah*!

Surat al-Fatihah is mentioned twice, being called *"al-mathaanee,"* repeated two times. In the prayers you read it two times because it was revealed two times, once in Mecca and once in Madinah. That is why it is called *"al-mathaanee,"* the only *surah* revealed to the Prophet ﷺ twice. Why it was revealed two times we will discuss later. Was the second time different from the first time? Yes, of course. Does the first time carry a different *tajalli* than the second time? Yes, and these *tajalliyaat* were given to the Prophet ﷺ and *awliyaullah* were able to extract some of these knowledges, which we will explain later *inshaa-Allah.*

The verses of *Surat al-Fatihah* are seven and the doors of Hellfire are seven; anyone who reads it will close these doors. The evidence is when Jibreel ؑ said to the Prophet ﷺ, *Yaa Muhammad! kuntu akhsha al-`adhaab `alaa ummatik,"I was worried that your ummah would be punished because of too many sins."* Are we living in a time without sins or are there too many sins? You cannot walk in the streets because there is so much *haraam*! Even the small stores sell alcohol, and even to enter a grocery store that sells alcohol is *haraam,* but don't all of us enter these stores? This is just an example, and there are so many other sins that we don't want to mention; everywhere you look these days is filled with *haraam.* So Jibreel ؑ said, "I was worried that your *ummah* would fall into *haraam,* but when *Surat al-Fatihah* was revealed I felt safe for them because I know what *Surat al-Fatihah* is carrying."

Prophet ﷺ wanted his *ummah* to know about this, so he asked Jibreel ؑ, *"Limaa,* why?"

Jibreel ؑ replied, "Because Allah said (19:71), (15:43)."

وَإِن مِّنكُمْ إِلَّا وَارِدُهَا كَانَ عَلَى رَبِّكَ حَتْمًا مَّقْضِيًّا

Not one of you but will pass over it: this is, with thy Lord, a Decree which must be accomplished. *(Surah Maryam, 19:71)*

وَإِنَّ جَهَنَّمَ لَمَوْعِدُهُمْ أَجْمَعِينَ

And verily, Hell is the promised abode for them all! *(Surat al-Hijr, 15:43)*

Here it says Hellfire has seven doors:

لَهَا سَبْعَةُ أَبْوَابٍ لِّكُلِّ بَابٍ مِّنْهُمْ جُزْءٌ مَّقْسُومٌ

To it are seven gates. For each of those gates is a (special) class (of sinners) assigned. *(Surat al-Hijr, 15:44)*

That is our destination that was promised, that Hellfire has seven doors and they are for everyone. Yes, there are seven doors, but when *Surat al-Fatihah* came, for anyone who reads it, it closes all of them. How is Allah ﷻ going to send you to Hellfire when He revealed to the Prophet ﷺ that we can close these doors by saying *"Bismillahi 'r-Rahmani 'r-Raheem"* and reciting *Surat al-Fatihah*? Each *ayah* locks those doors!

Sayyidina Jibreel ﷺ continued, *"Yaa Rasoolullah*! No now I feel the *ummah* is safe, because everyone can read *Surat al-Fatihah* and it becomes like armor that covers these doors. By this means, your *ummah* will pass through Hellfire safely, moving along the coverings over every door of Hellfire."

Sayyidina Hasan ؓ said, *"Rasoolullah* ﷺ said, 'Whoever reads *Surat al-Fatihah* once, it as if he thoroughly read the four Holy Books, the *Tawrat, Injeel, Zaboor* and Holy Qur'an!" *Allahu Akbar!*

May Allah ﷻ forgive us and may Allah bless us, and *inshaa-Allah* tomorrow we will see with what we will continue, because today I was going to mention one thing and it went this way instead. I didn't sit on the chair, because with discussing *Surat al-Fatihah* we cannot sit high, we have to sit lower.

We ask Allah ﷻ to give us from the Prophet ﷺ the manifestation of humbleness.

May Allah ﷻ forgive us and may Allah ﷻ bless us.

Wa min Allahi 't-tawfiq, bi ḥurmati 'l-ḥabīb, bi ḥurmati 'l-Fātiḥah.

And with Allah is success. For the sake of the Beloved, for his sake we recite the opening chapter of Holy Qur'an.

The Fifteen Meems of Surat al-Fatihah

Aʿūdhu billāhi min ash-Shayṭāni 'r-rajīm. Bismillāhi' r-Raḥmāni 'r-Raḥīm. Nawaytu 'l-arbāʿīn, nawaytu 'l-ʿitikāf, nawaytu'l-khalwah, nawaytu 'l-ʿuzlah, nawaytu 'r-riyāḍa, nawaytu 's-sulūk, lillāhi Taʿalā fī hādhā 'l-masjid. Atīʿūllāha wa atīʿū 'r-Rasūla wa ūlī 'l-amri minkum.

Obey Allah, obey the Prophet, and obey those in authority among you. (4:59)
Dastūr, madad yā Sulṭān al-Awlīyā, Mawlana Shaykh Nazim al-Haqqani ق.
Dastūr, madad yā Sulṭān al-Awlīyā, Mawlana Shaykh ʿAbdAllah ad-Daghestani ق.

As we said in the previous session, *Surat al-Fatihah* has a lot of secrets in it that Allah ﷻ mentioned to Prophet ﷺ, and the Prophet ﷺ mentioned, "Whoever reads *Surat al-Fatihah* once, it is as if he has read the different Holy Books, *az-Zaboor, at-Tawraat, al-Injeel, al-Qur'an* (Psalms, Old Testament, New Testament and the Qur'an)."

It is said that one of the names of *Surat al-Fatihah* is *al-Maahiyya,* "the One that Erases." Erases what? It erases everything that is bad, it erases all your sins, all bad characters, all power of your ego and all that is related to Shaytan, even if you don't feel it being erased! That is because it has fifteen "*meems*" in it. *Surat al-Fatihah* consists of 125 letters and every letter has a meaning. So every one of these fifteen "*meems*" has a meaning that is an ocean of knowledge, of which you cannot count the beginning or end because it relates to the Divine Presence! *Surat al-Fatihah* is Allah's ﷻ Divine Words, so there is no beginning or end to the reward and benefit you get from it!

So here we will make a little aside, *entre parentheses* (between parentheses); it begins with *Bismillahi 'r-Rahmani 'r-Raheem.* Some scholars say *Bismillahi 'r-Rahmani 'r-Raheem* is part of *Surat al-Fatihah,* and others say it is not. Whether a part of it or not, *Bismillahi 'r-Rahmani 'r-Raheem* is a Divine Word that contains *Ismullahi 'l-`Azham,* Allah's Greatest Name. Not one *wali* or *nabi* ﷺ knew that Name, except the Prophet ﷺ and until now, no one knows what that Name is.

Sayyidina Musa ﷺ asked Allah ﷻ to teach him *Ismullahi 'l-`Azham,* Allah's Greatest Name, and Allah said "no" because Sayyidina Musa ﷺ wanted to know that Name in order to give the order, *kun fayakoon,* "'Be!'

and it will be." That Name includes *khalq* in it, the ability to create, just as the first verse revealed to the Prophet ﷺ:

قرَأ بِاسْمِ رَبِّكَ الَّذِي خَلَقَ

Read! In the Name of your Lord Who created. *(Surat al-`Alaq, 96:1-2)*

Therefore, *Ismullahi 'l-`Azham* is the Name that is able to create, so when we write *"Bismillahi,"* the *"Alif"* is gone: it has to be *"b-ismi-Llah,"* as no one can carry the *Alif,* so Allah hides it. That letter represents Him and it is always *al-`izza lillah* and *kibriyya,* arrogance and pride, which are for Him Alone. So since no one carry that it is taken away, and only *"bismi"* is left.

So why did the *"ba"* take that responsibility? Because it is always in *sajda* to *"Alif,"* which is standing and *"ba"* is laying down. *"Ba"* did not agree when they put the dot (*nukta*) above it; all other Arabic letters accepted the dot to be above because they are proud, but *"ba"* didn't accept because it represents humility and, therefore, the Prophet ﷺ. You see it carries everything in its form, and the center of it is that dot under it! Allah gave the Prophet ﷺ the honor to be the *"ba."* So when you say *"Bismillah,"* it means, "By the Greatest Name of Allah," so it went into the secret of that Name that no one knows except the Prophet ﷺ, because he is the *"ba."* We will discuss this further, but here I wanted to explain that the *"Basmala"* carries a lot of heavy knowledge in it and the secret of Creation is in it (*Bismillahi 'r-Rahmani 'r-Raheem*), because it contains *Ismullahi 'l-`Azham.*

Allah gave to the Prophet ﷺ *`Uloom al-Awwaleen wa 'l-Aakhireen,* Knowledge of the First and Lasts, which is why they say about the *awaa'il as-soowar,* the beginning of every *surah* has the Greatest Name in it, and the *Basmala* has the *Ismullahi 'l-`Azham.* And Grandshaykh, may Allah bless his soul, acquired this knowledge when he was in seclusion for one year and they gave him a bowl of lentils daily, which he never ate it; he only drank water and tea. In Rashadiyya, now named Gunekoy, he did five years' seclusion and every day he only ate a piece of bread half the size of your hand, and seven olives. He emerged slim, like a stick.

He taught the head of Muslim scholars in the Middle East, my uncle, Shaykh `Abdullah (not Shaykh Mukhtar, he surrendered) who had seven questions to pose to Grandshaykh ق as a test. However, Grandshaykh didn't give him a chance to ask them, he just gave a three-hour *suhbah;* I was there and recorded it. My uncle, Shaykh `Abdullah, is a walking encyclopedia so he cannot bow to anyone, and he wanted to test

Grandshaykh ق. Once I visited my uncle when he was correcting the Arabic of a huge book, and I asked him what it was. He said, "I don't know, but they sent it to me to correct the Arabic."

I said, "What is that?"

He said, "It is the Bible!"

So one of the my uncle's questions was, "What is the Greatest Name of Allah?"

Without him asking the question, Grandshaykh ق opened the subject of *Ismullahi 'l-`Azham* and said, "In this time Allah has opened for the Prophet ﷺ to open something from it to *awliyaullah.*"

My uncle was astonished! When he entered he had shaken Grandshaykh's hand, but when he left he kissed it and later said to us, "If I were to write about what the Shaykh said, I could make a book from every word!" I cannot mention what Grandshaykh ق said about *Ismullahi 'l-`Azham* because it carries a lot.

The *"ba"* in *Bismillah* represents the beginning of Creation, so it carries the Creation that will be created, and *"meem"* represents what will appear in the Creation, in Muhammad ﷺ and represents the Prophet ﷺ. *Surat al-Fatihah* has fifteen *"meems."* So now we return to the discussion of *Surat al-Fatihah,* and this knowledge was revealed Grandshaykh ق from the secret of the *meems* from Muhiyyudeen ibn `Arabi ق.

السابعة من أسمائها الماحية لأن فيها خمسة عشر ميما بالبسملة فإذا قرأها العبد خرجت الممات كالطيور فتتعلق بالعرش فيثقل على الحملة فيقولون ربنا ما هذا الثقل فيقول هذا ثواب سورة قرأها عبدي فتقول الممات ربنا زدنا فيقول عشرين فيقولون ربنا زدنا فيزيدهم مائة وعشرين سيئة لكل ميم فتكون الجملة ألفا وثمانمائة سيئة تمحى لقارئها في الصلوات الخمس في كل يوم وليلة ثلاثون ألفا وستمائة سيئة

If you recite that, the 'meems' will manifest as birds of different shape and come out. (*Talkhees al-Ma`arif* by Muhammad `Arif)

Awliyaullah say that no one can carry the appearance of the Prophet ﷺ, so the first to appear is symbolized by a green bird that they can see, and then from the green bird it opens.

From the secret of the *meems* from Muhiyyudeen ibn `Arabi ق, Grandshaykh ق said in the *Basmala* from the *Fatihah* and from the fifteen *meems* that Jibreel ﷺ said, *"Yaa Rabbee,* show me Your *Mulk*!"

Allah ﷻ said, "When you descend with the Revelation you use two wings," and it is known from many *ahadith* that in fact, Jibreel ؑ has 600 wings. So He said, "Open all your wings!"

When *Maseeh al-Dajjal* comes, and we are now in the Last Days during which he will arrive, he will conquer the whole world except Mecca, Madinah and Sham. When he arrives in Sham, Allah ﷻ will order Jibreel ؑ to put his wing from Mt. Qasyoun along the road to Douma through the valley, and the Anti-Christ will reach there and think he has reached the end of *dunya*! Allah will stretch Sham to contain all Muslims, whoever believes in *tawheed*, the *muwwahidoon*. When Mahdi ؑ comes he will recite, "*Allahu Akbar*! *Allahu Akbar*! *Allahu Akbar*!" and the war will stop, and each believer will find himself moved to Sham in one second by angels with "*Bismillahi 'r-Rahmani 'r-Raheem*." That is the time of *khawaariq*. There's no need to book a ticket, one or three months before, because it is the time of miracles, and all computers and electronics will fail. So be happy, as the heavenly computers will take over!

Each "*meem*" corresponds to a secret of the Prophet ﷺ, of the knowledge that manifests itself as a green bird, so when Jibreel ؑ said, "O my Lord! Show me Your *Mulk*!" and Allah said, "Open your 600 wings and go with your full speed from this place!" Because the universes and Heavens are created, Jibreel ؑ began to move with full speed. Grandshaykh ق said he flew 70,000 heavenly years and he got tired, stopped and said, "*Yaa Rabbee*! Is it finished?"

Then Allah ﷻ replied, "*Yaa* Jibreel! You have not yet moved across one corner, you are still in one of the corners!"

Jibreel ؑ could see in front of him, with his powerful vision he can see the whole universe and even above it in one look, and he looked with all his power and was able to see an ocean of very small, white crystal dust grains and in the middle of that ocean of crystals he saw a green tree on top of which there was a green bird. That bird descended every second, picked up one crystal, ascended to the top of the tree and swallowed it.

Jibreel ؑ asked, "*Yaa Rabbee*! Who is that bird?"

Allah ﷻ replied, "Each grain of crystal is one universe, and each universe is like a grain of dust compared to the Greatness that I gave to the Prophet ﷺ. Every grain is a whole Creation with all that is in it, and Muhammad is the Messenger for all of them! All the other Prophets' job is finished; they were for this Adam, and he is the Messenger for all these creations."

That is how small the universe is compared to the Greatness of the Prophet ﷺ! In our eyes the universe is huge, but in the Prophet's ﷺ Vision the universes are like grains. Five years ago they said there are 6,000 galaxies, now they say there are millions of galaxies, and who knows how many stars; they say there are 80 billion stars in our galaxy, but it might be 80 trillion. They cannot see them, we cannot see them, but they know there are billions of galaxies. Don't say this is based on imagination, no! If you think like that, know that Allah ﷻ is Greater, He has more than that! Whatever you make of *t`azheem an-Nabi,* the Greatness of the Prophet ﷺ, still the Prophet ﷺ is above that, and whatever you say is the number of galaxies, you may say it is millions, still Allah ﷻ creates more than that, in the trillions! Whatever you think, Allah ﷻ is giving more!

The fifteen *meems* fly like birds, and go directly under *`Arsh ar-Rahman,* where every *mu'min* who sleeps on *wudu* after reciting three *Ikhlaas, Falaq, Naas* and *Surat al-Fatihah,* his soul will be making *sajda* under *`Arsh ar-Rahman*. The *meems* will be there, hanging onto *al-`Arsh*. There were eight angels created to carry the Throne by Allah's Order:

وَالْمَلَكُ عَلَىٰ أَرْجَائِهَا وَيَحْمِلُ عَرْشَ رَبِّكَ فَوْقَهُمْ يَوْمَئِذٍ ثَمَانِيَةٌ

And the angels will be on its sides, and eight will, that Day, bear the Throne of thy Lord above them. *(Surat al-Haqqah, 69:17)*

He created them because all the angels of Paradise were unable to carry it; then these eight angels became proud that they, rather than all other angels, were able to carry the Throne, when that pride entered their hearts, Allah made the Throne heavier than before so they could not carry it, and they were going to fall and then the *`Arsh ar-Rahman* was carrying them! So He said, "Who carries whom?" No one can carry the *`Arsh ar-Rahman*! Allah carries by, *Kun faya koon*.

Every *mu'min* makes *sajda* under the *`Arsh* at night when he sleeps. We continue from what Muhiyyudeen ibn al-`Arabi wrote:

> And the *meems* come running to *`Arsha ar-Rahman* and hold onto It. Then the eight angels say, *Rabbanaa maa haadha thiqqah?* "What is that *thiqqah,* heaviness, we never felt It heavy like that before?" Allah ﷻ replies, *Fayaqooloo t`aalaa, "Haadha thawwaabu suratun qara'a `abdee."* "This is the reward of the reading of one *surah,*" which is *Surat al-Fatihah,* "by My Servant!" Then the *meems* will speak, and each *meem*

has a secret. They speak because they represent the knowledge the Prophet ﷺ is giving: *Fataqool al-meemaat*, "*Rabbanaa maa jazaa'u man qara'naa?*" The *meems* will say, "O our Lord, what is the reward for those who read us?" *Fayaqooloo Allahu ta`alaa*, "*Intalliq kullu meemin tamhu `ashra sayyi'aat,*"

Allah said, "Go, and every *meem* will erase ten sins." *Fayaqooloon*, "*Rabbanaa zidnaa!*"

Then they say, "O our Lord! Increase for us!" *Fayazeedahum il al-mi'a wa l-`ishreen, thumma yazdaadoonaa fayazeedahum `ishreena `ishreen, fatakoonu 'l-jumlatu dhaalika alfa wa thamaani mi'a sayyi'a tumhaa li-qaari'haa, fi's-salawaat il-khams fee kulli yawmi wa layla, thalaathoon alf wa sita mi'at saiyyat*. And Allah increases it so each may erase 120 sins, then He increases until the total is 1800 sins are erased for every recitation of *Surat al-Fatihah*, as it is recited in the five prayers: twice in *Fajr*, four times in *Zhuhr*, four times in `*Asr*, three times in *Maghrib*, and four times in `*Isha*, which is seventeen times, so it will be in total 30,600 *hasanah*, each of which is bigger than this universe with all that is in it!

(*Talkhees al-Ma`arif* by Muhammad `Arif)

About the reward of reading *Surat al-Fatihah*, Sayyidina Muhiyyudeen ibn `Arabi ق said that Anas ibn Malik ؓ said the Prophet ﷺ told him:

I give an oath by Allah ﷻ that Jibreel ؑ told me, "Mikaa`il ؑ told me that the one who blows the Trumpet, Israfeel, told me that Allah ﷻ told him, 'By My Greatness and My *Tajalli* of Majesty and My Generosity, whoever reads one time '*Bismillahi 'r-Rahmani 'r-Raheem*' connected with *Fatihat al-Kitaab* in one breath, you witness that I have forgiven him! I will accept his good deeds and give him all the rewards and will take away all his sins. I will not punish his tongue with fire, and I will save him from the punishment of the grave and punishment of Hellfire, and on Judgment Day I will save him from the Greatest Fear, and he will come to Me as he is from *Ummat an-Nabi* ﷺ, and he will come to Me before all other *ummahs*, and *Ummat an-Nabi* ﷺ will enter Paradise first.'" (*Talkhees al-Ma`arif* by Muhammad `Arif)

And that is why Grandshaykh ق and Mawlana Shaykh Nazim ق say to read *Fatihah* in one breath, and that is how Allah will treat someone who recites *Surat al-Fatihah* once!

Shaykh Ahmad al-Tijani ق, a famous *wali*, said, "As for *Surat al-Fatihah*, the Prophet ﷺ related to me in a vision that each time you read it there is one *khatm* of the Holy Qur'an."

And it is said that *Surat al-Fatihah* equals one-third of the Holy Qur'an, so reading three *Surat al-Fatihah* is like reading the entire Holy Qur'an. Three *"Qul Huwa Allahu Ahad"* is like reading the entire Holy Qur'an.

Like Sayyidina Ismail al-Bukhari ﵁ who, before adding a hadith to the *Sahih*, would have to see the Prophet ﷺ in dream, Shaykh Ahmad al-Tijani ق said, "Whoever reads *Surat al-Fatihah* once, it is as if in one recitation you read all the *tasbeeh* of all that Allah ﷻ created from beginning to end!"

Look how much the *awliyaullah* gave us of food ready to eat, because we have a lot of sins, and look at how much *fadaa'il* we are getting without our knowledge! People don't know, but all this is written for us, whoever does these things, whether we know or not! And I quote:

Ahmad al-Tijani ق asked the Prophet ﷺ, *Fahal yahsal fee hadhal thawwab?* "Is that really what happened, that you will be as if you have made the *tasbeeh* of all Creation? Prophet ﷺ replied, *fa qaala Rasoolullah* ﷺ, *akthar min dhaalik!* "No, this is yet nothing! It is more than that. What you are describing to me of your vision is small compared to what Allah ﷻ will give." (There are 125 letters of *Surat al-Fatihah*.) He said, *Wa yahsal litaliya fee kulli marratin bi `adadi huroofiya wa l-huroofi 'l-Qur'an bi kulli harfin sab`aa kushoor!* "For every letter of the *Fatihah* you will get seven palaces, which are seven Heavens because each palace is a Heaven." (Quoted from *Talkhees al-Ma`arif* by Muhammad `Arif)

Not only that, but *Surat al-Fatihah* is *as-saba` al-mathaanee, wal-qur'an al-`azheem*, so it is separate from Holy Qur'an, which has about 321,075 letters, and for every letter they will get a piece of Paradise, *Rawdatan min riyaad al-Jannah*, for one recitation! So let's recite it now:

بِسْمِ اللهِ الرَّحْمَنِ الرَّحِيمِ الحَمْدُ للهِ رَبِّ العَالمِينَالرَّحْمنِ الرَّحِيم مَالِكِ يَوْمِ الدِّينِ إِيَّاكَ نَعْبُدُ وإِيَّاكَ نَسْتَعِين اهدِنَـــا الصِّرَاطَ المُستَقِيم صِرَاطَ الَّذِينَ أنعَمتَ عَلَيهِمْ غَيرِ المَغضُوبِ عَليهِمْ وَلاَ الضَّالِّينَ

A`oodhu billah mina 'sh-Shaytani 'r-rajeem. Bismillahi 'r-Rahmani 'r-Raheem. Alhamdulillahi Rabbi 'l-`alameen. Ar-Rahmani 'r-Raheem. Maaliki yaawmi 'd-deen. Iyyaka na`abudu wa iyyaka nasta`een. Ihdina 's-siraat al-mustaqeem. Siraat al-ladheena an`amta `alayhim. Ghayri 'l-maghdoobi `alayhim wa laa dhaaleen. Ameen. SadaqAllahu 'l-`Azheem.

Now you got all the benefits mentioned! In the footnotes of this book, the author says they used a computer to count the number of letters in the Holy Qur'an from a CD of *Qur'an al-Kareem*. The computer was able to precisely count the exact number of letters in the Holy Quran: 330,733. If you multiply what we said by the seven palaces of Paradise and the pieces of Paradise that Allah will give you for each letter, the quarters of Heavens the computer counted, it is a number you cannot read: 4,786,063,900 (four billion, 786 million, 63 thousand, nine hundred)! (Quoted from *Talkhees al-Ma`arif* by Muhammad `Arif, page 169). You cannot count; who is going to count?

Allah ﷻ said:

لَقَدْ أَحْصَاهُمْ وَعَدَّهُمْ عَدًّا

He does take an account of them (all) and has numbered them (all) exactly.

(Surah Maryam, 19:94)

And each one is coming to Him on the Day of Judgment and each reward that is coming to you is presented by Allah ﷻ. You counted four billion, 786 million, 63 thousand, nine hundred! Each one will intercede for who is granted that reward, so be happy that you are from *Ummat an-Nabi* ﷺ, as Allah gave a lot to *Ummat an-Nabi* ﷺ!

May Allah ﷻ forgive us and may Allah ﷻ bless us.

Wa min Allahi 't-tawfiq, bi ḥurmati 'l-ḥabīb, bi ḥurmati 'l-Fātiḥah.

And with Allah is success. For the sake of the Beloved, for his sake we recite the opening chapter of Holy Qur'an.

The Power of A`oodhu Billahi Min ash-Shaytani 'r-Rajeem

Aʿūdhu billāhi min ash-Shayṭāni 'r-rajīm. Bismillāhi' r-Raḥmāni 'r-Raḥīm. Nawaytu 'l-arbāʿīn, nawaytu 'l-ʿitikāf, nawaytu'l-khalwah, nawaytu 'l-ʿuzlah, nawaytu 'r-riyāḍa, nawaytu 's-sulūk, lillāhi Taʿalā fī hādhā 'l-masjid. Atīʿūllāha wa atīʿū 'r-Rasūla wa ūlī 'l-amri minkum. Obey Allah, obey the Prophet, and obey those in authority among you. (4:59)

Dastūr, madad yā Sulṭān al-Awlīyā, Mawlana Shaykh Nazim al-Haqqani ق.
Dastūr, madad yā Sulṭān al-Awlīyā, Mawlana Shaykh ʿAbdAllah ad-Daghestani ق.

Allahuma salli `alaa Sayyidina Muhammad* ﷺ *wa `alaa aali Sayyidina Muhammad ﷺ. In the previous session we spoke of the rewards that Allah ﷻ gives to the one who recites *Surat al-Fatihah* along with the *Basmalah*, either separately or connected. There is more on this issue, so *inshaa-Allah* we can explain more in the coming sessions, but this is only to prepare us for some interpretations given by many scholars and *awliyaullah* on the verses of Holy Qur'an.

There are both literal *tafaseer* and interpretational *tafaseer* of Holy Qur'an. We will try to shed some light on these spiritual (interpretational) *tafseers* that were explained by numerous friends of Allah ﷻ, whom He described in the Holy Qur'an:

ألا إِنَّ أَوْلِيَاء اللّهِ لاَ خَوْفٌ عَلَيْهِمْ وَلاَ هُمْ يَحْزَنُونَ

Behold! Verily on the friends of Allah there is no fear, nor shall they grieve.

(Surat al-Yunus, 10:62)

Saints of Allah have nothing to be sad about, because whatever they ask of Allah He will give, and they are following the footsteps of Allah, Who said:

إن كُنتُمْ تُحِبُّونَ اللّهَ فَاتَّبِعُونِي يُحْبِبْكُمُ اللّهُ وَيَغْفِرْ لَكُمْ ذُنُوبَكُمْ وَاللّهُ غَفُورٌ رَّحِيمٌ

Say (O Muhammad), "If you (really) love Allah, then follow me! Allah will love you and forgive your sins, and Allah is Oft-Forgiving, Most Merciful.

(Surat Aali-`Imraan, 3:31)

If you really want to love Allah ﷻ, you must follow Sayyidina Muhammad ﷺ. The *awliyaullah* follow the footsteps of the Prophet ﷺ step-by-step. If the Prophet ﷺ is asking from Allah for his *ummah* to be clean, what is the duty of *awliyaullah*? It is to ask for Allah to save his followers. If he is only sitting, eating, and drinking and not working hard for those who are taking his hand, why is he a *wali*?

Grandshaykh ق said, "Are *awliyaullah* in need of their followers, or are the followers in need of the *wali*?" An `*alim* says the followers are in need of the *wali*. Actually, the *wali* is in need of the followers, Because of the followers, on the Day of Promises, Allah wrote them to be guided by him, so his job is to guide them to the Prophet ﷺ, and the Prophet ﷺ will present the whole *ummah* to Allah ﷻ.

وَالرَّاسِخُونَ فِي الْعِلْمِ يَقُولُونَ آمَنَّا بِهِ كُلٌّ مِّنْ عِندِ رَبِّنَا

And those who are firmly grounded in knowledge say, "We believe in the Book; the whole of it is from our Lord." *(Surat Aali-`Imraan, 3:7)*

Raasikhoon are like mountains firmly planted like heavy anchors. We explained mountains as "pegs that make everything stable," as when the earth was not balanced Allah sent mountains to stabilize it. So the *awliyaullah* are pegs, well-established, anchored, who say, "*Yaa Rabbee*! We believe everything is from you!" Here, what is "everything"? The secrets of the Holy Qur'an come to them one-by-one for their followers.

فَإِذَا قَرَأْتَ الْقُرْآنَ فَاسْتَعِذْ بِاللهِ مِنَ الشَّيْطَانِ الرَّجِيمِ

Fa idhaa qiraat al-qur`an fasta`idh billaahi min ash-shaytani 'r-rajeem.

When you read the Holy Qur'an, you must ask support from Allah against Shaytan, the accursed. *(Surat an-Nahl, 16:98)*

That is why you see many *muqri'een* recite, "*A`oodhu billahi min ash-Shaytaani 'r-rajeem. Bismillahi 'r-Rahmaani 'r-Raheem*" and then the verses, and they skip the *Basmala,* but the *adab* is to recite, "*A`oodhu billahi min ash-Shaytaani 'r-rajeem. Bismillahi 'r-Rahmaani 'r-Raheem*" and then *Basmala* and then the verses.

When you enter a house, you go through the door and first you must knock on the door. If you knock Allah will open, but in His Way, not in your way, so you must knock! Ahmad al-Badawi ق knocked at the door to teach him how to knock with *adab,* discipline. Don't knock on the door saying, "O my Lord, open the door for me!" Who are you to say that? *Awliyaullah* are following the footsteps of the Prophet ﷺ, who never asked for himself but only for the *ummah.*

So *adab* is to say, *"A`oodhu billahi min ash-Shaytaani 'r-rajeem. Bismillahi 'r-Rahmaani 'r-Raheem."* That is asking Allah to take Shaytan away from you. Here, "Shaytan" refers to the four enemies that everyone has in their heart and *nafs,* the lower self or ego, is the first enemy. At the time or prayer, the *nafs* tells you to delay it. This happens to us from a lack of *imaan.* To destroy the *nafs* you must say, "I seek refuge in You, *yaa Rabbee,* from lack of *imaan*!" Without *imaan,* how do you destroy the self? If you really have *imaan* you can come against the desire of the self. *Alhamdulillah* you are not lazy to come here; I am lazy, but you are not lazy!

So first is knocking at the door and asking Allah ﷻ to destroy the four enemies, *fa idhaa qaraati 'l-qur`an fasta`idh billaahi min ash-shaytani 'r-rajeem.*

Does Shaytan only come when you read Holy Qur'an? Yes, Shaytan comes especially then, so it means you must decide not to allow *dunya* to enter your heart as you cannot have two in your heart. If you really show *hudoor,* presence, ask Allah to take away Shaytan and keep you in the presence of Allah ﷻ, the Prophet ﷺ, and *mashaykh.*

First, to get there you need *mahabatallah, mahabbat al-rasool, mahabbat al-mashaykh,* love of Allah, love of the Prophet ﷺ and love of *mashaykh.* So at that time you must focus and have *taamul:*

إِنَّ فِي خَلْقِ السَّمَاوَاتِ وَالأَرْضِ وَاخْتِلاَفِ اللَّيْلِ وَالنَّهَارِ لآيَاتٍ لِّأُوْلِي الألْبَابِ الَّذِينَ يَذْكُرُونَ اللّهَ قِيَامًا وَقُعُودًا وَعَلَىَ جُنُوبِهِمْ وَيَتَفَكَّرُونَ فِي خَلْقِ السَّمَاوَاتِ وَالأَرْضِ رَبَّنَا مَا خَلَقْتَ هَذا بَاطِلاً سُبْحَانَكَ فَقِنَا عَذَابَ النَّارِ

Inna fee khalqi 's-samaawaati wa 'l-ard wa'khtiflaafi 'l-layli wa 'n-nahaar la-ayaatin li-ooli 'l-albaab. Alladheena yadhkuroonallaha qiyaaman wa qu`oodan wa `alaa junoobihim wa yatafakkaroona fee khalqi 's-samawaati wa 'l-ard rabbanaa maa khalaqta hadha baatilan subhaanaka faqinaa `adhaab an-naar.

Behold! In the creation of Heaven and Earth, and in the alternation of night and day, there are indeed signs for men of understanding, those who remember Allah (always, and in prayers) standing, sitting and lying down on their sides, and contemplating the creation of the Heavens and the Earth, (saying), "Our Lord! You have not created (all) this without purpose! Glory to You! Give us salvation from the torment of the Fire." *(Surat Aali `Imraan, 3:191-192)*

And Allah ﷻ said, "We protect the Holy Qur'an from any alteration."

إِنَّا نَحْنُ نَزَّلْنَا الذِّكْرَ وَإِنَّا لَهُ لَحَافِظُونَ

Verily, We sent down the dhikr and surely, We will guard it (from corruption). *(Surat al-Hijr, 15:9)*

So when reciting you must also contemplate, then Allah will open the door that no one can open by himself. So when we say, "*A`oodhu billahi min ash-Shaytaani 'r-rajeem. Bismillahi 'r-Rahmaani 'r-Raheem,*" we are asking to destroy our self that is riding on everyone. We believe this, but we don't act on it; to act is to surrender to Allah ﷻ, not showing any will.

So next is *dunya,* and when you want to read Holy Qur'an you leave *dunya. Fa idhaa qaraati 'l-qur`an fasta`idh billaahi min ash-shaytani 'r-rajeem.* You have to leave *dunya* at that time. When you open Holy Qur'an to read, telephones ring, people come asking questions, and Shaytan will not leave you to really focus when reading Holy Qur'an because at that time you are entering the ocean of meditation, which is a huge threat to Shaytan!

تفكر ساعة خير من عبادة سبعين سنة

Tafakkarru sa`atin khayrun min `ibaadati saba`een sannah.

To remember Allah ﷻ (contemplate or meditate) for one hour is better than seventy years of worship.

When you are reciting Holy Qur'an and completely enter the state of contemplation and *tafakkur,* Allah will reward you as if you worshipped seventy years!

You can finish reading Holy Qur'an in one day if you read a *juz* in twenty minutes. He calculated it as 20 hours or say 24 hours. So as if you read the whole Holy Qur'an, *tafakkur sa`at,* if you contemplate one hour, it is like worshipping 70 years by reading Holy Qur'an for one hour. To really go into recitation of Holy Qur'an, you must enter into contemplation and leave *dunya*; enter the ocean and reality where Allah ﷻ is waiting to dress you, but to enter you have to leave your desires. When you read Holy Qur'an, cut everything around you and then your pleasures are only for Allah ﷻ.

The fourth enemy within us is Shaytan, who was first an angel named Azazeel. When he disobeyed, Allah turned him into Shaytan by cursing him. *Shayateen* have wives and children, and some interpretations say they get married, give birth and don't die.

الْخَبِيثَاتُ لِلْخَبِيثِينَ وَالْخَبِيثُونَ لِلْخَبِيثَاتِ

Women impure are for men impure, and men impure for women impure.

(Surat an-Noor, 24: 26)

The bad ones marry each other: *Iblees* and *Ibleesa* are famous and they marry and get children, but they don't die because Allah ﷻ postponed *Iblees'* death until the end of this *dunya*. Allah gave him opportunity as he asked, "Give me life so I can mislead all of them (humans)!" And so Shaytan doesn't die. Any human being who acts like Shaytan is *maradat al-jinn*. Some *mu'min jinn* marry and die. At the beginning, *Iblees* was an angel, so at the beginning they had angelic power but Allah cursed them and turned it to the *shaytanic* power of fire. But *jinn* marry and they die. The *kaafir jinn* work with *shayateen al-ins*, the bad human beings. Shaytans don't want to work with anyone because they are so powerful. And the *maradat al-jinn*, the most tough of *jinn*, work with human beings that dress the character of the *jinn* who are *kuffaar*. And they take from the *shayateen* and that is why they are able to do black magic, to harm men and women, like the two angels in the kingdom of Sulayman عليه السلام.

وَاتَّبَعُوا مَا تَتْلُوا الشَّيَاطِينُ عَلَى مُلْكِ سُلَيْمَانَ وَمَا كَفَرَ سُلَيْمَانُ وَلَـكِنَّ الشَّيَاطِينَ كَفَرُوا
يُعَلِّمُونَ النَّاسَ السِّحْرَ وَمَا أُنزِلَ عَلَى الْمَلَكَيْنِ بِبَابِلَ هَارُوتَ وَمَارُوتَ وَمَا يُعَلِّمَانِ مِنْ أَحَدٍ حَتَّى
يَقُولاَ إِنَّمَا نَحْنُ فِتْنَةٌ فَلاَ تَكْفُرْ فَيَتَعَلَّمُونَ مِنْهُمَا مَا يُفَرِّقُونَ بِهِ بَيْنَ الْمَرْءِ وَزَوْجِهِ وَمَا هُم بِضَآرِّينَ
بِهِ مِنْ أَحَدٍ إِلاَّ بِإِذْنِ اللّهِ وَيَتَعَلَّمُونَ مَا يَضُرُّهُمْ وَلاَ يَنفَعُهُمْ وَلَقَدْ عَلِمُواْ لَمَنِ اشْتَرَاهُ مَا لَهُ فِي
الآخِرَةِ مِنْ خَلاَقٍ وَلَبِئْسَ مَا شَرَوْاْ بِهِ أَنفُسَهُمْ لَوْ كَانُواْ يَعْلَمُونَ

They followed what the evil ones gave out (falsely) against the power of Solomon. The blasphemers were, not Solomon, but the evil ones, teaching men magic and such things as came down at Babylon to the angels Harut and Marut. But neither of these taught anyone (such things) without saying, "We are only for trial; so do not blaspheme." They learned from them the means to sow discord between man and wife, but they could not thus harm anyone except by Allah's permission and they learned what harmed them, not what profited them. And they knew that the buyers of (magic) would have no share in the happiness of the Hereafter. And vile was the price for which they did sell their souls, if they but knew! (Surat al-Baqarah, 2:102)

They teach what will harm families, men and women. So yes, *sihr* exists and is black magic. They did black magic against the Prophet ﷺ, so they can also do black magic against *shuyookh*, especially some Egyptians and Moroccans, Gulf Arabs, Africans, and in North and South America. Everywhere there are people who do *sihr* to destroy family ties and to destroy love between *shaykh* and student. They blow on the food to make it poison and offer it to *shuyookh*, *`ulama* and everyone. So if the Prophet ﷺ was affected by *sihr*, cannot *shuyookh* also be affected? Presidents? Can it not it be done on anyone? So what to do? Knock on the door by saying, "A`oodhu billahi min ash-Shaytaani 'r-rajeem. Bismillahi 'r-Rahmaani 'r-Raheem," and for certain there are specific words to read, but in general we read "A`oodhu billahi min ash-Shaytaani 'r-rajeem. Bismillahi 'r-Rahmaani 'r-Raheem" to destroy *sihr*.

When the magicians came against Sayyidina Musa ؑ they brought snakes, but he brought a real snake that ate up all their *sihr* snakes and when they witnessed that power, they believed in the Lord of Sayyidina Musa ؑ and Haroon ؑ. Some forms of *sihr* is too harmful, and therefore, some have been authorized to take it away. Mawlana Shaykh Nazim ق gave us that power. *Inshaa-Allah* soon we will give something to read, to understand what is *sihr*. So knock and enter the Door of the King of Kings! If you want to visit the king, can you enter without permission? So when you want to enter, you cannot jump inside from the window or they will arrest you as a trespasser! You have to enter through the door, which also has a lock, whose key is "A`oodhu billahi min ash-Shaytaani 'r-rajeem. Bismillahi 'r-Rahmaani 'r-Raheem, I am seeking refuge in Allah, *billah*, "by Allah."

If Allah ﷻ doesn't open we will be stranded outside between the hands of Shaytan! To open the lock you have to be clean and pure, which is why you cannot read the Holy Qur'an and be impure. Unfortunately, and many people put Holy Qur'an on the floor, which is disrespect to Allah's Ancient Divine Words! So whoever wants to read Holy Qur'an, which is Allah's Words and Allah's *Dhikr*, if you call Him by any words, for example, "Alif. Lam. Meem," when you recite like that you are entering *munajaat*, a heavenly conversation, which you want to be a genuine conversation, not mixed with ego. So who will take you there? When you decide to read Holy Qur'an, there are angels assigned to take you to *Munajaat al-Habeeb*, not just the conversation, but the Divine Presence, where you will be in a full state of love, approaching Him by His Own Words!

If someone wrote a book and heard only a paragraph of it recited, he will be so happy! Therefore, what do you think if someone is given the opportunity to read Allah's Divine Words? It is honor and pride for us to open the Holy Qur'an and read! If some people don't know how to read Arabic, they may only look at the pages and there is Light coming from the Arabic. That is *adab* with the One you love. *Adab* is to have what He gave you always between your hands.

So what is needed when you enter there? To have complete purity of *wudu* and to pray two *raka`ats* of *wudu,* and then recite Holy Qur'an. You have to purify your tongue, which can take you to Hellfire! Through that tongue you express your feelings. Some people use it to mock others and come against everyone to show they are higher. So we have to take refuge in Allah by saying, "*A`oodhu billahi min ash-Shaytaani 'r-rajeem. Bismillahi 'r-Rahmaani 'r-Raheem,*" and then you enter the conditions to read Holy Qur'an, which removes Shaytan and his bad manners! So when you recite, "*A`oodhu billahi min ash-Shaytaani 'r-rajeem. Bismillahi 'r-Rahmaani 'r-Raheem,*" any sin you previously committed will be waived completely! When you say, "*A`oodhu billahi min ash-Shaytaani 'r-rajeem. Bismillahi 'r-Rahmaani 'r-Raheem,*" it means, "I am seeking refuge in Allah from Shaytan, the rejected," and then whatever wrong Shaytan tempted you to do before that is forgiven, and you are taken the treasures of *Bismillahi 'r-Rahmani 'r-Raheem*!

Allah ﷻ said:

وَأَوْفُوا بِعَهْدِي أُوفِ بِعَهْدِكُمْ وَإِيَّايَ فَارْهَبُون

Fulfill your promise to Me and I will fulfill My promise to you, and fear none but Me. *(Surat al-Baqara, 2:40)*

"I created you *`abd*, servant, so I fulfilled the promise and it is now a requirement for you to fulfill your promise. I gave to you and you are My *`abd*. Even if the angels do something wrong, I curse them. Then you become Shaytan, and there is no forgiveness for them. So the biggest weapon against your biggest enemy is to recite, '*A`oodhu billahi min ash-Shaytaani 'r-rajeem. Bismillahi 'r-Rahmaani 'r-Raheem'* and I will come immediately to your rescue because I promised!"

Say, *"A`oodhu billahi min ash-Shaytaani 'r-rajeem. Bismillahi 'r-Rahmaani 'r-Raheem,"* and, "You are The One with Perfect Generosity because You said, 'If you call Me I will give you.'"

There are three levels when you say, *"A`oodhu billahi min ash-Shaytaani 'r-rajeem. Bismillahi 'r-Rahmaani 'r-Raheem." Kalimat al-isti`adha,* "the Words of (Seeking) Refuge" are three: *sifaatiyya afa`aliyya wa dhaatiyya.*

The Prophet ﷺ said:

اللهم إني أعوذ برضاك من سخطك وأعوذ بمعفاتك من عقوبتك وأعوذ بك منك . لا
أحصي ثناء عليك أنت كما أثنيت على نفسك

I seek refuge in You from You being angry with me, and secondly I seek refuge in Your Cure from Your punishment, and then I seek refuge in You by You; no one praised You as You praised Yourself. *(Muslim, Tirmidhi)*

This is the way the Prophet ﷺ explained *'A`oodhu billahi min ash-Shaytaani 'r-rajeem. Bismillahi 'r-Rahmaani 'r-Raheem.'*

May Allah ﷻ forgive us and may Allah ﷻ bless us.

Wa min Allahi 't-tawfiq, bi ḥurmati 'l-ḥabīb, bi ḥurmati 'l-Fātiḥah.

And with Allah is success. For the sake of the Beloved, for his sake we recite the opening chapter of Holy Qur'an.

Allah's Protection

Aʿūdhu billāhi min ash-Shayṭāni 'r-rajīm. Bismillāhi' r-Raḥmāni 'r-Raḥīm.
Nawaytu 'l-arbāʿīn, nawaytu 'l-ʿitikāf, nawaytu'l-khalwah, nawaytu 'l-ʿuzlah,
nawaytu 'r-riyāḍa, nawaytu 's-sulūk, lillāhi Taʿalā fī hādhā 'l-masjid.
Atīʿūllāha wa atīʿū 'r-Rasūla wa ūlī 'l-amri minkum.
Obey Allah, obey the Prophet, and obey those in authority among you. (4:59)

Dastūr, madad yā Sulṭān al-Awlīyā, Mawlana Shaykh Nazim al-Haqqani ق.
Dastūr, madad yā Sulṭān al-Awlīyā, Mawlana Shaykh ʿAbdAllah ad-Daghestani ق.

Allahumma salli `alaa Sayyidina Muhammad, hatta yarda Sayyidina Muhammad! Salloo `alaa an-Nabi ﷺ. Yesterday we explained, *"A`oodhu billahi min ash-Shaytani 'r-rajeem. Bismillahi 'r-Rahmani 'r-Raheem,"* and the continuation to *Surat al-Fatihah.*

وَإِنْ أَحَدٌ مِّنَ الْمُشْرِكِينَ اسْتَجَارَكَ فَأَجِرْهُ حَتَّى يَسْمَعَ كَلاَمَ اللّهِ ثُمَّ أَبْلِغْهُ مَأْمَنَهُ ذَلِكَ بِأَنَّهُمْ قَوْمٌ لاَّ يَعْلَمُونَ

(If someone) asks you for asylum, grant it to him so that he may hear the Word of Allah, then escort him to where he can be secure.

(Surat at-Tawbah, 9:6)

We said, "When someone asks for your protection, you have to give them asylum." If anyone runs to you from an evil power that is destroying their home and life, what will you do? Anyone will protect him. And then, "If he comes to you, remind him of Allah's Words and then take him to a safe haven."

When you say, *"A`oodhu billahi min ash-Shaytani 'r-rajeem. Bismillahi 'r-Rahmani 'r-Raheem,"* who are you saying it to? The One Who revealed the *ayah* to the Prophet ﷺ, which instructs us to take care of whomever comes to us for asylum and to teach him Allah's Words. After he listens to Allah's Words and accepts, then take him to a safe haven where he will be protected from anyone who might be following him. If anyone goes to a king seeking asylum, do you think he will not protect them? Of course he would! So if you run to Allah ﷻ seeking refuge, what will happen? It means He is teaching us some hints so we can be safe. Allah ﷻ tells us to say, *"A`oodhu billahi min ash-Shaytani 'r-rajeem,"* and He will save us from His Punishment as He does not really want to punish anyone, so He instructs us to say this, which then takes us to a safe haven where Shaytan has no power.

Allah ﷻ is *Maalik al-Mulook,* The King of Kings. *Mulook* can die, but only the Real King can live forever. Only Allah ﷻ is that and He can live forever! Say, "Allah! He is the One Who exists!" Everyone else has no existence, but we cannot say that for the Prophet ﷺ, as he existed in Allah's Presence before any Creation, so he is Divine as he is from *Noorillah! Huwa 'n-noor yahdi 'l-haa'ireen...* (from Qasida) He is the Light that guides like a beacon on the seashore or at the airport that guides those who are confused about where to go. On the Day of Judgment, he will be the shade, the shade of the Messenger of Allah ﷺ!

If you knock at the door, Allah ﷻ tells us to ring the bell. Here in New York they have a bell, they press a button to ring it, and everyone is happy! Why are they happy when they charge you money for it? They are taking their money and are like parasites sucking their blood, living on people's money, but people are happy with their bell. That is the bell of Shaytan, while the bell of Allah ﷻ is *"A`oodhu billahi min ash-Shaytani 'r-rajeem."* He is the King of Kings and The One who says:

يَوْمَ هُم بَارِزُونَ لَا يَخْفَى عَلَى اللَّهِ مِنْهُمْ شَيْءٌ لِّمَنِ الْمُلْكُ الْيَوْمَ لِلَّهِ الْوَاحِدِ الْقَهَّارِ

The Day whereon they will (all) come forth; not a single thing concerning them is hidden from Allah. Whose will be the Dominion that Day? That of Allah, The One, The Irresistible! *(Surat al-Ghaafir, 40:16)*

He is the One who glorifies Himself by Himself! In this *ayah* He asks, "To whom is the kingdom today?" He is not asking you to answer, He is answering Himself to His Honor. He is not in need of our answers! *Nafsahu bi-nafsi,* He glorifies Himself by Himself! No one can glorify Allah ﷻ the way He glorifies Himself, as He mentions in the Qur'an:

سُبْحَانَ الَّذِي أَسْرَى بِعَبْدِهِ لَيْلاً مِّنَ الْمَسْجِدِ الْحَرَامِ إِلَى الْمَسْجِدِ الأَقْصَى الَّذِي بَارَكْنَا حَوْلَهُ لِنُرِيَهُ
مِنْ آيَاتِنَا إِنَّهُ هُوَ السَّمِيعُ الْبَصِيرُ

Glory be to He Who transported His Servant by night from the Inviolable House of Worship (at Mecca) to the Remote House of Worship (at Jerusalem), the environs of which We had blessed so that We might show him some of Our symbols, for verily He Alone is All-Hearing, All-Seeing. *(Surat al-Israa', 17:1)*

In this *ayah,* Allah ﷻ is praising Himself by Himself, as there is no way you can understand the *Mi`raaj* and so to show that this is something extraordinary, above miracles and beyond universes, Allah ﷻ said, *subhaanee ma `azhama shaanee,* "Glory be to Me! I am the Greatest! No one can know Me!" *laa tudrikahu 'l-absaar wa huwa yudriku 'l-absaar,* there is no way to see Him with our eyesight or in a vision, nor to even understand about Him! But He can reach anyone from among His Creation: angels, *jinn,* human beings and all else that He created.

It is mentioned in many *ahadith* and sayings of the *Sahaabah* ؓ that Allah ﷻ sends revelation to the bee regarding where to go and find its nectar. Allah ﷻ reveals to the bee which flower to go to in order to find its food. Scientists say a bee can fly up to 400 km to reach its food, and it also knows the way there and the return. We say, they know the way through Divine Revelation and they can smell where their queen bee is and they follow that light to reach there, because light emits from the hive. Honey is *shifa'a,* as imentioned in the Qur'an:

يَا أَيُّهَا النَّاسُ قَدْ جَاءَتْكُم مَّوْعِظَةٌ مِّن رَّبِّكُمْ وَشِفَاءٌ لِّمَا فِي الصُّدُورِ وَهُدًى وَرَحْمَةٌ لِّلْمُؤْمِنِينَ

O Mankind! There has come to you a guidance from your Lord and a healing for (the diseases) in your hearts, and for those who believe a guidance and a mercy. (Surat Yunus, 10:57)

يَخْرُجُ مِن بُطُونِهَا شَرَابٌ مُّخْتَلِفٌ أَلْوَانُهُ فِيهِ شِفَاءٌ لِّلنَّاسِ

There issues from within the bodies of the bee a drink of varying colors, wherein is healing for Mankind. (Surat an-Nahl, 16:69)

Allah ﷻ has put a cure for human beings in honey, not only for the physical body, but also the spiritual body. That is why it is recommended to take a spoon of honey every day.

So He answered Himself by Himself, saying *subhaanee ma `azhama sha'anee,* "Glory be to Me! How great is My Greatness!" Allah ﷻ says this about Himself, which means there is no one great except Allah ﷻ! Allah is Great and everyone else is insignificant! Also, Allah ﷻ only dressed the Prophet ﷺ from His Greatness for him to reach *Qaaba Qawsayni aw Adnaa;* otherwise, he would not have been able to reach there.

Don't you think if you knock on Allah's Door that He will give you refuge? What are you running away from evil and sins to knock on the door of *hasanaat*. When you knock on the Door of *al-Kareem*, the Generous One, do you think He will say, "No, I don't want you here?" He is *al-Qaadir*, The One With Absolute Power, and all things are under His Command, so you are going to The One Who can save you!

In an *ayah* of the Holy Qur'an, Allah ﷻ has asked us to come to Him from *kullu 'l-maqdooraat*, "everything destined." He said if we come to Him, He will erase all He wrote as our destiny and give us what we want, and He will even erase His Will! Allah ﷻ erases whatever He likes; even if He puts you in Hellfire and you run to Him, He will save you from it and put you in Paradise, but only if you come to Him! All He says is, "Come to Me!" and He will save you from *jami`ee makhaawaf wa 'l-aafaat*, all that you fear: afflictions, difficulties and problems.

It is said of all of the *`uloom* , knowledges, of how to come, *fafirroo 'ilaa-Allah*, to run toward Allah ﷻ, to go in and open that door, are in these two words: *"a`oodhu billah."* Every knowledge of how to run to Allah is contained in that! Allah ﷻ says:

فَفِرُّوا إِلَى اللَّهِ إِنِّي لَكُم مِّنْهُ نَذِيرٌ مُّبِينٌ

Run (away immediately) to Allah (from harm)! Verily, I am from Him a Warner to you, clear and open. *(Surat az-Zaariyat, 51:50)*

Run to Allah, *fafirroo 'ilaa-Allah* and He will dress you in *`uloom al-kutub al-arb`a*, the Knowledge of the four different Holy Books. Although you might not know how to know them, in *Akhirah* you will appear in front of Allah ﷻ as an *`alim* in that, carrying all that knowledge because He dressed you in that. It's like if someone gave you a *jubba* and you keep it, wear it all the time and might not take it off, because it is safe haven for you. So if you are running to Allah ﷻ, He will dress you with that knowledge, but your tongue is frozen to speak those knowledges because it is veiled in the heart. All the knowledges of *`uloom al-kutub al-arb`a* are in the Qur'an because it came to wrap everything in Islam. *Inna ad-deena `indallahi al-Islam,* "The religion with Allah is Islam," so everything is in that Qur'an, and if you read more and more Holy Qur'an you get more and more understanding of the verses.

Recently in Nelson, the *imam* recited this *ayah* at *Fajr*:

يَا أَيُّهَا الْمُزَّمِّلُ ۞ قُمِ اللَّيْلَ إِلَّا قَلِيلًا نِصْفَهُ أَو انْقُصْ مِنْهُ قَلِيلًا أَوْ زِدْ عَلَيْهِ وَرَتِّلِ الْقُرْآنَ تَرْتِيلًا إِنَّا سَنُلْقِي عَلَيْكَ قَوْلًا ثَقِيلًا
إِنَّ نَاشِئَةَ اللَّيْلِ هِيَ أَشَدُّ وَطْءًا وَأَقْوَمُ قِيلًا إِنَّ لَكَ فِي النَّهَارِ سَبْحًا طَوِيلًا وَاذْكُرِ اسْمَ رَبِّكَ وَتَبَتَّلْ إِلَيْهِ تَبْتِيلًا

O thou folded in garments! Stand (in prayer) by night, but not all night, half of it or a little less or a little more, and recite the Qur'an in slow, measured, rhythmic tones. Soon shall We send down to you a weighty Message. Truly the rising by night is most potent for governing (the soul), and most suitable for (framing) the Word (of prayer and praise). True, there is for you by day prolonged occupation with ordinary duties, but keep in remembrance the Name of your Lord and devote yourself to Him wholeheartedly.

(Surat al-Muzzamil, 73:1-8)

I will not explain in detail, but here Allah ﷻ addresses the Prophet ﷺ, saying, *Yaa ayyuhaa 'l-muzzammil. Qumi 'l-layla illa qaleelaan,* "O, the one covered up! Wake up during the night and pray." It means to remain awake for worship the whole night except a small part of it. This was the first Divine Order to the Prophet ﷺ, then Allah reduced it to either half the night until midnight, "or make it less or more." *Wa rattili 'l-quraana,* "and during this time, read the Holy Qur'an." *Wa adhkur ismi rabbika.* I said to the Imam at Nelson that when I heard this *ayah*, it was as if I had never heard it or read it before! At that moment, something special in that *ayah* came to me. We were discussing this in *Majalis ash-Dhikr*, so you can find what I said in the previous *suhbah*, because I want you to go back and look for it!

Wa 'dhkur ismi rabbika: Allah ﷻ is telling you to remember Him by mentioning His Name; "*Isma rabbika*" is Allah, "say the Name of your Lord!" So He says, *Qul Allah! Idhkurnee bi ismee!* "Say 'Allah!' Remember my Name!" And unfortunately, some Muslims wrongfully say, "Don't make *dhikr* of 'Allah,' make *dhikr* with '*laa ilaaha illa-Llah.*'" Okay, "*laa ilaaha illa-Llah*" is the Declaration of *Maqaam at-Tawheed*, but Allah is the Ocean of Witnessing, *mushahadah*, and when you mention Allah's Name, He will give you everything from that Name, the Highest Name, *al-Ism al-`Azham*, that we don't know. All the Prophets asked for it, and Sayyidina Musa ؏ also asked Allah ﷻ to give him that and He didn't, but He gave it to the Prophet ﷺ.

So this is what came, the secret of *Ism al-`Azham,* Allah's Greatest Name! Allah ﷻ will dress you with that secret although you don't know it is there, because it his veiled. He will upload that to you and on the Day of Judgment He will download it from you. You will come with that *noor!* There, you will appear to people like Prophets, shining like a star on a dark night on the Day of Resurrection!

That is why *awliyaullah* can be seen. These sessions are under the name of Sultan al-Awliya Mawlana Shaykh Nazim ق and Sultan al-Awliya Grandshaykh `AbdAllah ق and they will not let us down. They are our lawyers on the Day of Judgment! They will present us to the Prophet ﷺ and we will be under their wings! Every morning when they make *Salaat an-Najaat,* all their *mureeds* pass in front of them one-by-one in every *sajda* and they present them to the Prophet ﷺ!

All the four Holy Books are contained in the Qur'an, and all the knowledge of the Qur'an is in *Surat al-Fatihah.* When you seek refuge in Allah, He will open for you the Secret of *Bismillah,* and the first letter of the *Basmala* is in the *'ba'* and so you cannot get the knowledge except from the *'ba,"* which ' is Sayyidina Muhammad ﷺ! The first verse revealed to the Prophet ﷺ was:

اقْرَأْ بِاسْمِ رَبِّكَ الَّذِي خَلَقَ

Read! In the Name of your Lord Who created. *(Surat al-`Alaq, 96:1-2)*

Read in the Name of Your Lord! There are many Beautiful Names and Attributes, so which Name to read? Read in the Name of Allah ﷻ! If you read in the Name of the Creator, you know the *khalq* and what He created. Why did Allah ﷻ say, *"rabbika al-ladhee khalaq."* Of course, the Prophet ﷺ knows that Allah ﷻ is the Creator, but Allah ﷻ wants him to open that Door, to enter into that ocean, to take from it and dress the *ummah* until the Day of Judgment.

So in Whom are we seeking refuge? In *al-Kareem,* in the Generous One! Will He not take us to safety? And He will give you a safe haven from Shaytan, so what does that make you? It makes you a *wali!* What makes *awliyaullah* to be *awliya*? Of course, they have been granted that by Allah ﷻ, but also they run away from Shaytan to Allah ﷻ! We aren't speaking about the physical body now, because we are still under sins, but they give that to you and they leave it with the Prophet ﷺ as a trust, then when you are ready they give you the code to open it and take. They are not in need of it; they are not hoarding it not like us, but they save it and give to the *ummah* when it is needed.

So by saying, *"A`oodhu billah,"* you fulfill the requirements of *fafirroo 'ilaa-Allah,* run to Allah! We fulfill the order, *"Ati`oollaaha!"* We run to Allah ﷻ by saying, *"A`oodhu billahi min ash-Shaytaani 'r-rajeem."* It will be written for us that Allah ﷻ has taken us to a safe haven away from Shaytan and then you will be shining, clean and dressed with all kinds of Allah's Beautiful Names and Attributes.

May Allah ﷻ forgive us and may Allah ﷻ bless us.

Wa min Allahi 't-tawfiq, bi ḥurmati 'l-ḥabīb, bi ḥurmati 'l-Fātiḥah.

And with Allah is success. For the sake of the Beloved, for his sake we recite the opening chapter of Holy Qur'an.

Islamic Calendar and Holy Days

The Islamic calendar is lunar-based, with twelve months of 29 or 30 days. A lunar year is shorter than a solar year, so Muslim holy days cycle back in the Gregorian (Western) calendar. This is how Ramaḍān is celebrated at different times of the year, as the annual Islamic calendar is ten days shorter than the Gregorian calendar.

Four Islamic months are sacred: Muharram, Rajab, Dhūl-Qʿadah and Dhūl-Hijjah. Holy months include "God's Month" (Rajab), "Prophet's Month" (Shaʿbān) and the "Month of the People" (Ramaḍān), in which pious acts are rewarded more generously.

Months of the Islamic Calendar

1. Muḥarram
2. Safar
3. Rabīʿ ul-Awwal (Rabīʿ I)
4. Rabīʿ uth-Thāni (Rabīʿ II)
5. Jumāda al-Awwal (Jumādi I)
6. Jumāda uth-Thāni (Jumādi II)
7. Rajab
8. Shaʿbān
9. Ramaḍān
10. Shawwāl
11. Dhū'l-Qʿadah
12. Dhū'l-Hijjah

al-Hijra

The 1st of Muharram marks the beginning of the Islamic New Year, chosen because it is the anniversary of Prophet Muḥammad's ﷺ historic *hijra* (migration) from Mecca to Madinah, where he established the first, preeminent Muslim community in which he introduced unprecedented social reforms, including civil law, human and women's rights, religious tolerance, taxation to serve the community, and military ethics.

ʿAshura

On 10th Muharram, ʿAshūra commemorates many sacred events, such as Noah's ark coming to rest, the birth of Abraham, and the building of the Kaʿbah in Mecca. ʿAshūra is a major holy day, marked with two days of fasting, on the 9th/10th or on 10th/11th based on a holy tradition (*ḥadīth*) of Sayyīdinā Muḥammad ﷺ.

Mawlid

Mawlid al-Nabī, 12th Rabiʿ al-Awwal, commemorates Prophet Muḥammad's birth in 570. Mawlid is celebrated globally throughout this month in huge communal gatherings in which a famous poem "Qasīdah al-Burdah" is recited, accompanied by drummers, illustrious poetry recitals, religious singing, eloquent sermons, gift giving, feasts, and feeding the poor. Most Muslim nations observe Mawlid as a national holiday.

Laylat al-Isra wal-Mi'raj

Literally, "the Night Journey and Ascension;" 27th of Rajab is when Sayyīdinā Muḥammad ﷺ physically traveled from Mecca to Jerusalem, ascended in all the levels of Heaven from a rock in the Dome of the Rock, and returned to Mecca—while his bed was still warm. In the Night Journey, Islam's five daily prayers were ordained by God. Sayyīdinā Muḥammad ﷺ also prayed with Abraham, Moses, and Jesus in Jerusalem's al-Aqsa Mosque, signifying that Muslims, Christians, and Jews follow one god. This holy event designated Jerusalem as the third holiest site in Islam, after Mecca and Madinah.

Laylat al-Bara'ah

The "Night of Freedom from Fire" occurs on 15th Shaʿbān. On this night God's Mercy is great; hence, the night is spent reciting Holy Qurʿan and special prayers, as well as visiting the deceased.

Ramadan

Many regard Ramaḍān, the ninth month of the Islamic calendar, the holiest month of the year. Muslims observe a strict fast and participate in pious activities such as charitable giving and peace making. It is a time of intense spiritual renewal for those who observe it. Fasting is meant to instill social awareness of the needy, and to promote gratitude for God's endless favors. The fast is typically broken in a communal setting, and hence Ramaḍān is a highly social month. At night, a special Ramaḍān prayer known as "*Tarawīh*" is offered in congregation, in which one-thirtieth of the Holy

Qur'an is recited by the *imām* (prayer leader); thus the entire holy book of six thousand verses is recited in this month.

Eid al-Fitr

"Festival of Fast-Breaking" marks the end of Ramaḍān and is celebrated the first three days of Shawwāl. It is a time for charity and celebration with family and friends for completing a month of blessings and joy. In the Last Days of Ramaḍān, each Muslim family gives "Zakāt al-Fitr"(charity of fast-breaking) which consists of cash and/or food, to help the poor. On the first early morning of Eid, Muslims observe a special congregational prayer, such as Christmas/Easter Mass or the High Holy Days. After Eid prayer is a time to visit family and friends, and give gifts and money (especially to children). Many specialty foods and sweets are prepared solely for Eid days. In most Muslim countries, the entire three days of Eid is a national holiday.

Yawm al-Arafat

"Day of 'Arafat," 9 Dhul-Hijjah, occurs just before the celebration of Eid al-Adha. Pilgrims on Hajj assemble for the "standing" on the plain of 'Arafat, located outside Mecca, where they contemplate the Day of Standing (Resurrection Day). Muslims elsewhere in the world fast this day, and gather at a local mosque for prayers. Thus, those who cannot perform Hajj that year still honor the sacrifice of Abraham.

Eid al-Adha

The "Feast of Sacrifice," celebrated from the 10th-13th Dhul-Hijjah, marks Prophet Abraham's willingness to sacrifice his son Ismā'īl on God's order. To honor this event, Muslims perform Hajj, the pilgrimage to Mecca that is incumbent on every mature Muslim once in their life if they have the means. Celebrations begin with an animal sacrifice to commemorate Sayyīdinā Abraham's sacrifice. In Islam, he is known as *Khalilullāh,* "God's friend." Many consider him the first Muslim and a premiere role model, for his obedience to God and willingness to sacrifice his only child without even questioning the command.

Glossary

ʿabd (pl. *ʿibād*): lit. slave; servant.
ʿAbdAllah: Lit., "servant of God"
Abū Bakr aṣ-Ṣiddīq: the closest Companion of Prophet Muḥammad; the Prophet's father-in-law, who shared the *Hijrah* with him. After the Prophet's death, he was elected the first caliph (successor); known as one of the most saintly Companions.
Abū Yazīd/Bayāzīd Bistāmī: A great ninth century *walī* and a master of the Naqshbandi Golden Chain.
adab: good manners, proper etiquette.
adhān: call to prayer.
Ākhirah: the Hereafter; afterlife.
al-: Arabic definite article, "the".
ʿalāmīn: world; universes.
Alḥamdūlillāh: praise God.
ʿAlī ibn Abī Ṭālib: first cousin of Prophet Muḥammad, married to his daughter Fāṭimah; the fourth caliph.
Alif: first letter of Arabic alphabet.
ʿAlīm, al-: the Knower, a divine attribute
Allah: proper name for God in Arabic.
Allahu Akbar: God is Greater.
ʿāmal: good deed (pl. *ʿamāl*).
amīr (pl., *umarā*): chief, leader, head of a nation or people.
anā: first person singular pronoun
anbīyā: prophets (sing. *nabī*).
ʿaql: intellect, reason; from the root *ʿaqila*: lit., "to fetter."
ʿArafah, ʿArafat: a plain near Mecca where pilgrims gather for the principal rite of *Hajj*.
ʿarif: knower, Gnostic; one who has reached spiritual knowledge of his Lord.
ʿĀrifūnʿ bil-Lāh: knowers of God.
Ar-Raḥīm: The Mercy-Giving, Merciful, Munificent, one of Allah's ninety-nine Holy Names.
Ar-Raḥmān: The Most Merciful, Compassionate, Beneficent; the most repeated of Allah's Holy Names.
ʿarsh, al-: the Divine Throne.
aṣl: root, origin, basis.
astāghfirullāh: lit. "I seek Allah's forgiveness."
Awlīyāullāh: saints of Allah (sing. *walī*).
āyah (pl. *ayāt*): a verse of the Holy Qur'an.
Āyat al-Kursī: "Verse of the Throne," a well-known supplication from the Qur'an (2:255).
ʿAzraʿīl: the Archangel of Death.
Badīʿ al-: The Innovator; a divine name.
Banī Ādam: Children of Adam; humanity.
Bayt al-Maqdis: the Sacred Mosque in Jerusalem, built at the site where Solomon's Temple was later erected.
Bayt al-Mā'mūr: much-frequented house; this refers to the Kaʿbah of the Heavens, which is the prototype of the Kaʿbah on Earth, circumambulated by the angels.
bayaʿ: pledge; in the context of this book, the pledge of initiation of a disciple (*murīd*) to a Shaykh.
Bismillāhi'r-Raḥmāni'r-Raḥīm: "In the name of the All-Merciful, the All-Compassionate"; introductory verse to all chapters of the Qur'an, except the ninth.

Dajjāl: the False Messiah (Anti-Christ) will appear at the end-time of this world, to deceive Mankind with false divinity.
dalālah: evidence.
dhāt: self / selfhood.
dhawq (pl. *adhwāq*): tasting; technical term referring to the experiential aspect of gnosis.
dhikr: remembrance, mention of God in His Holy Names or phrases of glorification.
ḍīyā: light.
Diwān al-Awlīyā: the nightly gathering of saints with Prophet Muḥammad in the spiritual realm.
du'ā: supplication.
dunyā: world; worldly life.
'Eid: festival; the two major celebrations of Islam are 'Eid al-Fitr, after Ramaḍān; and 'Eid al-Adha, the Festival of Sacrifice during the time of *Hajj*, which commemorates the sacrifice of Prophet Abraham.
farḍ: obligatory worship.
Fātiḥah: Sūratu 'l-Fātiḥah; the opening chapter of the Qur'an.
Ghafūr, al-: The Forgiver; one of the Holy Names of God.
ghawth: lit. "Helper"; the highest rank of all saints.
ghaybu' l-muṭlaq, al-: the Absolute Unknown; known only to God.
ghusl: full shower/bath obligated by a state of ritual impurity, performed before worship.
Grandshaykh: generally, a *walī* of great stature. In this text, refers to Mawlana 'AbdAllah ad-Daghestāni (d. 1973), Mawlana Shaykh Nazim's master.
hā': the Arabic letter ه
ḥadīth Nabawī (pl., *aḥadīth*): prophetic *ḥadīth* whose meaning and linguistic expression are those of Prophet Muḥammad.
Ḥadīth Qudsī: divine saying whose meaning directly reflects the meaning God intended but whose linguistic expression is not divine speech as in the Qur'an.
ḥaḍr: present
Hajj: the sacred pilgrimage of Islam obligatory on every mature Muslim once in their life.
ḥalāl: permitted, lawful according to Islamic *Sharī'ah.*
ḥaqīqah, al-: reality of existence; ultimate truth.
ḥaqq: truth
Ḥaqq, al-: the Divine Reality, one of the 99 Divine Names.
ḥarām: forbidden, unlawful.
ḥasanāt: good deeds.
hāshā: God forbid.
ḥarf: (pl. *ḥurūf*) letter; Arabic root "edge."
Ḥawā: Eve.
ḥaywān: animal.
Hijrah: emigration.
ḥikmah: wisdom.
ḥujjah: proof.
hūwa: the pronoun "he,"made up of the Arabic letters *hā'* and *wāw*.
'ibādu 'l-Lāh: servants of God.
'ifrīt: a type of Jinn, huge and powerful.
iḥsān: doing good, "It is to worship God as though you see Him; for if you are not seeing Him, He sees you."
ikhlāṣ, al-: sincere devotion.
ilāh: (pl. *āliha*): idols or gods.
ilāhīyya: divinity.
ilhām: divine inspiration sent to *awlīyāullāh*.
'ilm: knowledge, science.

ʿilmu ʾl-awrāq: knowledge of papers.
ʿilmu ʾl-adhwāq: knowledge of taste.
ʿilmu ʾl-ḥurūf: science of letters.
ʿilmu ʾl-kalām: scholastic theology.
ʿilmun ladunnī: divinely inspired knowledge.
imān: faith, belief.
imām: leader of congregational prayer; an advanced scholar followed by a large community.
insān: humanity; pupil of the eye.
insānu ʾl-kāmil, al-: the Perfect Man, *i.e.*, Prophet Muḥammad.
irādatullāh: the Will of God.
irshād: spiritual guidance.
ism: name.
isma-Llāh: name of God.
isrāʿ: night journey; used here in reference to the night journey of Prophet Muḥammad.
Isrāʿfīl: Archangel Rafael, in charge of blowing the Final Trumpet.
jalāl: majesty.
jamāl: beauty.
jamaʿa: group, congregation.
Jannah: Paradise.
jihād: to struggle in God's Path.
Jibrīl: Gabriel, Archangel of revelation.
Jinn: a species of living beings created from fire, invisible to most humans. Jinn can be Muslims or non-Muslims.
Jumuʿah: Friday congregational prayer, held in a large mosque.
Kaʿbah: the first House of God, located in Mecca, Saudi Arabia to which pilgrimage is made and to which Muslims face in prayer.
kāfir: unbeliever.
Kalāmullāh al-Qadīm: lit., Allah's Ancient Words, *viz*. the Holy Qur'an.
kalīmat at-tawḥīd: lā ilāha illa-Llāh: "There is no god but Al-Lah (the God)."
karāmat: miracles.
khalīfah: deputy.
Khāliq, al-: the Creator, one of 99 Divine Names.
khalq: Creation.
khāniqah: designated smaller place for worship other than a mosque; *zāwiyah.*
khuluq: conduct, manners.
Kirāmun Kātabīn: honored Scribe angels.
lā: no; not; not existent; the particle of negation.
lā ilāha illa-Llāh Muḥammadun Rasūlullāh: There is no deity except Allah, Muḥammad is the Messenger of Allah.
lām: Arabic letter ل.
al-Lawḥ al-Maḥfūẓ: the Preserved Tablets.
Laylat al-Isrāʿ wa'l-Miʿrāj: the Night Journey and Ascension of Prophet Muḥammad to Jerusalem and to the Seven Heavens.
Madīnātu ʾl-Munawwara: the Illuminated city; city of Prophet Muḥammad; Madinah.
mahr: dowry, given by the groom to the bride.
malakūt: divine kingdom.
Malik, al-: the Sovereign, a divine name.
Mālik: Archangel of Hell.
maqām: spiritual station; tomb of a prophet, messenger or saint.
maʿrifah: gnosis.
Māshā'Allah: as Allah Wills.
Mawlānā: lit. "Our master" or "our patron,"referring to an esteemed person.

maẓhar: place of disclosure.
miḥrāb: prayer niche.
Mikāʿīl: Michael, Archangel of rain.
mīzān: the scale that weighs our deeds on Judgment Day.
mīm: Arabic letter م.
minbar: pulpit.
Miracles: of saints, known as *karamāt*; of prophets, known as *muʿjizāt* (lit., "That which renders powerless or helpless").
miʿrāj: the ascension of Prophet Muḥammad from Jerusalem to the Seven Heavens.
Muḥammadun rasūlu ʾl-Lāh: Muḥammad is the Messenger of God.
mulk, al-: the World of dominion.
Muʿmin, al-: Guarḍian of Faith, one of the 99 Names of God.
muʿmin: a believer.
munājāt: invocation to God in a very intimate form.
Munkir: one of the angels of the grave.
murīd: disciple, student, follower.
murshid: spiritual guide; *pir*.
mushāhadah: direct witnessing.
mushrik (pl. *mushrikūn*): idolater; polytheist.
muwwāḥid (pl. *muwāḥḥidūn*): those who affirm God's Oneness.
nabī: a prophet of God.
nāfs: lower self, ego.
Nakīr: the other angel of the grave (with Munkir).
nūr: light.
Nūḥ: the prophet Noah.
Nūr, an-: "The Source of Light"; a divine name.
Qādir, al-: "The Powerful"; a divine name.
qalam, al-: the Pen.
qiblah: direction, specifically, the direction faced by Muslims during prayer and other worship, towards the Sacred House in Mecca.
Quddūs, al-: "The Holy One"; a divine name.
qurb: nearness
quṭb (pl. *aqṭāb*): axis or pole. Among the poles are:
Quṭbu ʾl-Bilād: Pole of the Lands.
Quṭbu ʾl-Irshād: Pole of Guidance.
Quṭbu ʾl-Aqṭāb: Pole of Poles.
Quṭbu ʾl-Aʿdham: Highest Pole.
Quṭbu ʾl-Mutaṣarrif: Pole of Affairs.
al-quṭbīyyatu ʾl-kubrā: the highest station of poleship.
Rabb, ar-: the Lord.
Raḥīm, ar-: "The Most Compassionate"; a divine name.
Raḥmān, ar-: "The All-Merciful"; a divine name.
raḥmā: mercy.
rakaʿat: one full set of prescribed motions in prayer. Each prayer consists of a one or more *rakaʿats.*
Ramaḍān: the ninth month of the Islamic calendar; month of fasting.
Rasūl: a messenger of God.
Rasūlullāh: the Messenger of God, Muḥammad ﷺ.
Raʿūf, ar-: "The Most Kind"; a divine name.
Razzāq, ar-: "The Provider"; a divine name.
rawḥānīyyah: spirituality; spiritual essence of something.
Riḍwān: Archangel of Paradise.
rizq: provision; sustenance.
rūḥ: spirit. *Ar-Rūḥ* is the name of a great angel.
rukūʿ: bowing posture of the prayer.
ṣadaqah: voluntary charity.

Ṣaḥābah (sing., *ṣaḥābī*): Companions of the Prophet; the first Muslims.
ṣaḥīḥ: authentic; term certifying validity of a *ḥadīth* of the Prophet.
ṣāim: fasting person (pl. *ṣāimūn*)
sajda (pl. *sujūd*): prostration.
ṣalāt: ritual prayer, one of the five obligatory pillars of Islam. Also, to invoke blessing on the Prophet.
Ṣalāt an-Najāt: prayer of salvation, offered in the late hours of night.
ṣalawāt (sing. *ṣalāt*): invoking blessings and peace upon the Prophet.
salām: peace.
Salām, as-: "The Peaceful"; a divine name. *As-salāmu ʿalaykum:* "Peace be upon you," the Islamic greeting.
Ṣamad, aṣ-: Self-Sufficient, upon whom creatures depend.
ṣawm, ṣiyām: fasting.
sayyi'āt: bad deeds; sins.
sayyid: leader; also, a descendant of Prophet Muḥammad.
Sayyīdinā: our master (fem. *sayyidunā; sayyidatunā*: our mistress).
shahādah: lit. testimony; the testimony of Islamic faith: *lā ilāha illa ʾl-Lāh wa Muḥammadun rasūlu ʾl-Lāh,* "There is no god but Allah, the One God, and Muḥammad is the Messenger of God."
Shah Naqshband: Muḥammad Bahauddin Shah Naqshband, a great eighth century walī, and the founder of the Naqshbandi Ṭarīqah.
Shaykh: lit. "old Man," a religious guide, teacher; master of spiritual discipline.
shifāʿ: cure.
shirk: polytheism, idolatry, ascribing partners to God
ṣiffāt: attributes; term referring to Divine Attributes.
Silsilat adh-dhahabīyya: "Golden Chain"of spiritual authority in Islam
sohbet (Arabic, *suḥbah*): association: the assembly or discourse of a Shaykh.
subḥānAllah: glory be to God.
sulṭān/sulṭānah: ruler, monarch.
Sulṭān al-Awlīyā: lit., "King of the *awlīyā*; the highest-ranking saint.
Sūnnah: Practices of Prophet Muḥammad in actions and words; what he did, said, recommended, or approved of in his Companions.
sūrah: a chapter of the Qur'an; picture, image.
Sūratu ʾl-Ikhlāṣ: Chapter 114 of Holy Qur'an; the Chapter of Sincerity.
ṭabīb: doctor.
tābiʿīn: the Successors, one generation after the Prophet's Companions.
tafsīr: to explain, expound, explicate, or interpret; technical term for commentary or exegesis of the Holy Qur'an.
tajallī (pl. *tajallīyāt*): theophanies, God's self-disclosures, Divine Self-manifestation.
takbīr: lit. *"Allahu Akbar,"*God is Great.
tarawīḥ: the special nightly prayers of Ramaḍān.
ṭarīqat/ṭarīqah: lit., way, road or path. An Islamic order or path of discipline and devotion under a guide or Shaykh; Sufism.
taṣbīḥ: recitation glorifying or praising God.
tawāḍaʿ: humbleness.
ṭawāf: the rite of circumambulating the Kaʿbah while glorifying God during *Hajj* and ʿUmra.

tawḥīd: unity; universal or primordial Islam, submission to God, as the sole Master of destiny and ultimate Reality.
Tawrāt: Torah
tayammum: Alternate ritual ablution performed in the absence of water.
ʿubūdīyyah: state of worshipfulness. Servanthood
ʿulamā (sing. *ʿālim*): scholars.
ʿulūmu ʾl-awwalīna wa ʾl-ākhirīn: knowledge of the "Firsts" and the "Lasts" refers to the knowledge God poured into the heart of Prophet Muḥammad during his ascension to the Divine Presence.
ʿulūm al-Islāmī: Islamic religious sciences.
Ummāh: faith community, nation.
ʿUmar ibn al-Khaṭṭāb: an eminent Companion of Prophet Muḥammad and second caliph of Islam.
ʿumra: the minor pilgrimage to Mecca, performed at any time of the year.
ʿUthmān ibn ʿAffān: eminent Companion of the Prophet; his son-in-law and third caliph of Islam, renowned for compiling the Qur'an.
walad: a child.
waladī: my child.
walāyah: proximity or closeness; sainthood.
walī (pl. *awlīyā*): saint, or "he who assists"; guarḍian; protector.
wasīlah: a means; holy station of Prophet Muḥammad as God's intermediary to grant supplications.
wāw: Arabic letter و
wujūd, al-: existence; "to find," "the act of finding," and "being found."
Yʿaqūb: Jacob; the prophet.
yamīn: the right hand; previously meant "oath."
Yawm al-ʿahdi waʾl-mīthāq: Day of Oath and Covenant, a heavenly event before this Life, when all souls of humanity were present to God, and He took from each the promise to accept His Sovereignty as Lord.
yawm al-qiyāmah: Day of Judgment.
Yūsuf: Joseph; the prophet.
zāwiyah: designated smaller place for worship other than a mosque; also *khāniqah*.
zīyāra: visitation to the grave of a prophet, a prophet's companion or a saint.

Other Publications at www.isn1.net

Shaykh Muhammad Nazim Adil al-Haqqani

- We Have Honored the Children of Adam (2013)
- Heavenly Counsel: from Darkness into Light (2013)
- Heavenly Showers (2012)
- The Sufilive Series (6) (2010-12)
- Breaths from Beyond the Curtain (2010)
- In the Eye of the Needle
- Eternity: Inspirations from Heavenly Sources
- The Healing Power of Sufi Meditation
- In the Mystic Footsteps of Saints (2) (also in ebook format)
- Liberating the Soul (6)

Shaykh Muhammad Hisham Kabbani

- The Importance of Prophet Muhammad in Our Daily Life (2013)
- The Hierarchy of Saints (2013)
- The Heavenly Power of Divine Obedience and Gratitude (2013)
- Salawat of Tremendous Blessings (2012, *Turkish/Spanish*)
- The Dome of Provisions (2012)
- The Prohibition of Domestic Violence in Islam (2011/*Fatwa*)
- The Sufilive Series (6) (2010-12)
- Jihad: Principles of Leadership in War and Peace (2010)
- Cyprus Summer Series (2) (2009)
- The Nine-fold Ascent (2008)
- Who Are the Guides? (2008)
- Illuminations (2007)
- Banquet for the Soul (2006)
- Symphony of Remembrance
- The Healing Power of Sufi Meditation
- In the Shadow of Saints
- Keys to the Divine Kingdom
- The Sufi Science of Self-Realization (*also in French*)
- Universe Rising: the Approach of Armageddon?
- Pearls and Coral
- Classical Islam and the Naqshbandi Sufi Tradition
- The Naqshbandi Sufi Way
- Links of Light: The Golden Chain
- The Encyclopedia of Islamic Doctrine (7 volumes)
- Angels Unveiled, a Sufi Perspective
- Encyclopedia of Muḥammad's Women Companions and the Traditions They Related

Hajjah Amina Adil

- Muhammad: the Messenger of Islam (2001)
- The Light of Muhammad
- Lore of Light / Links of Light
- My Little Lore of Light (3 vol.)

Hajjah Naziha Adil Kabbani

- Heavenly Foods (2011)
- Secrets of Heavenly Food (2009)

www.ingramcontent.com/pod-product-compliance
Lightning Source LLC
Chambersburg PA
CBHW060458080526
44584CB00015B/1471
* 9 7 8 1 9 3 8 0 5 8 1 5 8 *